His Story in the Stars

By
Gary Hullquist

TEACH Services, Inc.
PUBLISHING
www.TEACHServices.com • (800) 367-1844

ISBN-13: 978-1-5725-8139-5 (Paperback)
Library of Congress Control Number: 98-86816

Published by

Contents

His Story in the Stars 7

Sun Worship 14

Zodiac 21

The Wanderers 29

Virgo, The Woman and Her Seed 37

Libra, Balancing the Scales 45

Scorpio 51

Sagittarius, The Archer 57

Aquarius, The Water-Bearer 67

Pisces 75

Aries, The Ram 81

Taurus, The Bull 89

The United Gemini 97

Cancer, The Crab 103

Leo, The Lion of the Tribe of Judah 111

The Twelve Celestial Signs and Their Decans 119

Preface

The heavens declare the glory of God;
  and the firmament sheweth His handywork,
Day unto uttereth speach,
  and night unto night sheweth knowledge,
There is no speech nor language,
  where their voice is not heard....
Their line is gone out through all the earth,
  and their words to the end of the world.

Psalm 19:1-4

There is a message in the sky. It is a message about God and His work. It is constant and continuous and all pervasive-transcultural, global, world wide. And it was written by God. "It is he that buildeth his stories in the heaven." *Amos 9:6* "I consider thy heavens, the work of thy fingers," David said, "the moon and the stars, which thou hast ordained;" *Psalm 8:3*. It should be of no surprise that God would capitalize on celestial splendor to make a statement. When You have the world's gaze, why not say something of strategic importance? Why not tell Your story when You have free advertising?

"Lift up your eyes on high, and behold who hath created these things, that bringeth out their host by number: He calleth them all by names...." *Isaiah 40:26* Adam may have named the animals, but God named the stars.

This study is a revision of several previous works on the subject. The materials presented here are drawn heavily from these pioneers. After all, "there is nothing new under the sun." Foremost recognition is given to Joseph A. Seiss and his *The Gospel in the Stars*, originally published in 1882. Although a detailed treatment, the language is verbose with an eloquence less suited for today's reader.

My desire is that you may gain a fresh appreciation for the infinite wisdom of our Creator. He is the source of all knowledge. But also realize that God has an Enemy who, under the cover of darkness, spreads tares among the wheat. The Adversary is determined to distort, confuse, pervert, wrest and twist divine truth at every possible opportunity. While sublime lessons were drawn by the Master Designer with the intent to display His Glory, Evil subverted such notions into the pseudoscience of astrology and its product the horoscope. May the rediscovery of God's original purpose strengthen your faith and confidence in His Word and *His Story in the Stars*.

His Story in the Stars

"And God said, Let there be lights in the firmament of the heaven to divide the day from the night; and let them be for signs, and for seasons, and for days, and years."

Genesis 1:14

"The invisible things of Him from the creation of the world are clearly seen, being understood by the things that are made."

Romans 1:20.

PISCES
PEGASUS
ANDROMEDA
ARIES
DELPHINIUS
SAGITTA
AQUILA
SWAN
CASSIOPEIA
PERSEUS
TAURUS
ORION
CEPHUS
LYRA
AURIGA
DRACO
URSA MINOR
GEMINI
HERCULES
LYNX
CORONA
CANIS MINOR
URSA MAJOR
SERPENS
BOOTES
CANCER
COMA
LEO
VIRGO

The stars, celestial luminaries of intergalactic space, were placed *for signs*—to represent something of *sign*ificance. The printed word is symbolic; alphabetic characters are signs representing sounds and numbers. Musical notation hosts a large array of signs and symbols indicating pitch and timing, but there is no literal relationship between these signs and the actual substance they represent. They are chosen, more or less, arbitrarily.

The plague of flies was a *sign* to the Egyptians of God's supremacy and power. *Exodus 8:22*. The retreating sun dial shadow was a *sign* to Hezekiah of healing and a reprieve from death. *II Kings 20:8–11*. So also, the patterns found in a star-studded sky are only representative of much more transcendent concepts, themes and spiritual truth. There is in the sky above a clear legible record for all to see of the Gospel story.

> "These orbs of light should be made to bear, express, record, and convey some special teaching different from what is naturally deducible from them." Seiss, *The Gospel In The Stars."*

As is so often the case, Evil distorts and obscures original truths wherever it can. The beauty of holiness becomes disguised by fable, myth and lie. The story of a Saviour becomes perverted into tales of Santa Clause and Superman. And astrology has totally eclipsed the original intention of the Creator's lesson in the sky.

Astrology perverted the lessons, intended to save mankind, into a means of predicting mundane events. Celestial bodies were changed from symbols of salvation into omens of fate inflicted by planetary conjunctions, equinoxes, eclipses, and lunar phases. The course of one's life was believed to be based on the position of the zodiacal signs at the moment of birth or even conception. Decisions about life could be made by following the signs.

The Magi of Matthew's Gospel, came seeking the King of the Jews in response to seeing His star. These Wisemen, traveling from eastern lands, were moved and led by a combination of astronomical signs and prophetic record. *Matthew 2:2*

> "There shall come a star out of Jacob, and a sceptre shall rise out of Israel," Baalim had prophesied years before. *Numbers 24:17*

Daniel pinpointed the time. *From the going forth of the commandment to rebuild Jerusalem to Messiah the Prince* was exactly 483 years. The appearance of a star in the east merely confirmed the promise of God.

> "When the fullness of the time was come, God sent forth His Son." *Galatians 4:4*

Stars have always been paramount emblems to human observers. They persist, unmoved, permanent fixtures, sublime monuments, visible in all lands as universal memorials to eternal truth. Would the God of creation overlook such an opportunity to speak to the human race? To provide humanity with *a glorious record of primeval faith and hope...a sublime testimony...an invincible attestation.*

Frescoes in the Sky

"The heavens declare the glory of God," *Psalm 19:1* but not merely because they *show His handiwork*. His glory is preeminently displayed in the condescension, incarnation, revelation, substitution and resurrection of Jesus Christ, His Son. The story of redemption, resplendent theme of Scripture, is also emblazoned in the heavens, found among the stars, tokens of *some primordial and sacred system of astronomy. Psalm 2:2.*

The Gospel Story in the Stars encompasses two chief themes: the Serpent and the Cross. The fall of man by *the Dragon, that old Serpent, called the Devil, and Satan Revelation 12:9* is addressed by a Mightier One from heaven who assumes human nature, suffers and dies in order to exalt the object of His care to the right hand of God, vanquishing the Dragon and becoming the Author of eternal salvation. This is the Everlasting Gospel carried by the first Angel flying in the midst of heaven of *Revelation 14*:6, 7.

Here, too, in Revelation the Serpent meets his end. He reared his head in Genesis, to beguile and deceive the whole world through Eve, but God intervened and cursed the Serpent,

> "Because thou hast done this...I will put enmity between thee and the woman, and between thy seed and her seed; it shall bruise thy head, and thou shalt bruise his heel."
>
> *Genesis 3:14,15*

This is the original story, the very first epic saga concerning a Dragon-slaying Saviour, preempting St. George by over 5 millennia. There, in the Garden, the conflict began, the match was set, the sides were drawn—the Dragon and the Deliverer, the Serpent and the Saviour, the Prince of Darkness and the Prince of Peace, the Devouring lion *seeking whom he may devour* and the Lion of the tribe of Judah *slain from the foundation of the world.* Deadly and malignant versus Divine and merciful. An *irreconcilable feud* promised to crush the Destroyer under the feet of a wounded Lamb *led as a sheep to the slaughter. The master theme of both Testaments, the chief substance of all prophecy and promise...written upon the stars...as an everlasting witness of God's gracious purposes toward our race. I Peter 5:8, Revelation 13:8, Isaiah 53:7.*

With an infinite number of lights among the starry realm, how can anyone conclude with certainty any meaning or pattern? Actually, only about 5,000 stars are visible to the unaided eye. Of these, only a few hundred of the brightest have received proper names. The seemingly erratic star patterns have been preserved as fossil relics of a primitive astrology. As early as 2,000 years BC, Sumerian cuneiform texts record the names of constellations still familiar to us today: the lion, the bull, the scorpion. Other occurrences of these symbols on prehistoric seals, vases and gaming boards suggest they may well have originated as early as 4000 BC. In China astronomical records featuring Virgo as the first sign were kept as early as the reign of Yao, placing them in possession of the antediluvian version of the Zodiac about twenty-three hundred years before Christ. This dates to before the time of Abraham. A number of configurations follow the same themes known to the West, such as the scorpion, lion, dipper and hunter (Orion), "suggesting the possibility of a very old common tradition." *Encyclopedia Britannica 2:225, 1984 Edition*

Abram, according to Josephus, "was the first who ventured to publish this notion that there was but one God, the creator of the universe." This opinion "was derived from the irregular phenomena that were visible both at land and sea; as well as those that happen to the sun and moon, and all the heavenly bodies." Josephus then quotes Berosus the ancient Babylonian historian in referencing Abram: "In the tenth generation after the flood, there was among the Chaldeans a man, righteous and great, and skillful in the celestial science." Later, when Abram vacationed in Egypt, "He communicated to them arithmetic, and delivered to them the science of astronomy...for that science came from the Chaldeans into Egypt, and from thence to the Greeks also." *Antiquities of the Jews Book 1, Chap. VII, VIII*

Homer in the 9th century BC mentions several constellations in his Odyssey where Odysseus is presented as:

> Gazing with fixed eye on the Pleiades,
> Boötes setting late and the Great Bear,
> By others called the Wain, which wheeling round,
> Looks ever toward Orion and alone
> Dips not into the waters of the deep.

Odyssey, V

In Elizabethan England the Great Bear (Big Dipper or Ursa Major) was still called Charle's Wain (wagon):

> An't be not four by
> The day I'll be hanged; Charles' Wain is over
> The new chimney and yet our horse not pack'd.

Shakespeare's King Henry IV,
Part I, Act II, Scene 1

Surprisingly, there is order and predictable arrangement in the star fields. The earliest account contained in the *Phaenomena* of Aratus, a poet of the 3rd century BC, named 43 star-groups or constellations. Cicero referenced him by name in his *De republica*, I, 14. Later, the list was expanded to 48 and included over a thousand stars ranked by 6 magnitudes of brightness and mapped according to their ecliptic coordinates by the 2nd century AD Alexandrian astronomer Claudius Ptolemaeus AKA Ptolemy in his best-seller the *Almagest*.

The constellations are formed along the ecliptic, that imaginary line traced by the Sun across the heavens as our planet makes its annual orbit. The Sun appears to move 30° every month or 360° a full circle in twelve. Moon and planets follow much the same path, a natural belt encircling the sky, as it deviates less than 10° from the solar ecliptic.

Though the ecliptic is fixed among the stars, the longitude of any particular star increases by 1.396° per century (a change of 28° since the time of Christ) due to the precessional movement of the equator. Consequently, Ptolmey's catalog included the Southern Cross and Centaurus (now out of view from the northern hemisphere having sunk below the southern horizon) but failed to mention the first magnitude star Achernar (now visible above the northern horizon).

Sun Worship

From the most ancient of times, earth's nearest star has been the object of wonder and worship. The oldest book of Scripture recognized the perversion of sun worship. Beholding "the sun when it shined, or the moon walking in brightness" was considered an iniquity because it denied "the God that is above." *Job 31:26*

The Chinese Temple of Heaven in Peking contains an altar to the sun. The cult of Mithra involved worship of the *sol invictus*. In Babylon, the sun god was *Shamash*. The Aztecs of the new world worshipped *Tonatiuh*. The Incas offered still-beating-hearts from live human sacrifices to their sun god *Inti* and placed mummies of their dead rulers in the sun temple of Cuzco. In Japan emperors were worshipped as descendants of the sun-goddess *Amaterasu*. Egypt revered the sun god *Ra* of Heliopolis (sun city) and worshipped their Pharaohs as the sons of Ra.

In *Deuteronomy 4:19* God provided his people with "statutes and judgments" and instructed Moses to teach them "Lest thou lift up thine eyes unto heaven, and when thou seest **the sun, the moon, and the stars**, even all the host of heaven, shouldest be driven to worship them." The second commandment of the decalogue specifically prohibits the worship of images and other gods. Unfortunately, the Bible record mentions numerous references to sun worship and its practice by even God's professed people.

Israel soon "worshipped all **the host of heaven**, and served Baal." *2 Kings 17:16;* in *Chapter 21:3-6* Manasseh "worshipped all **the host of heaven**, and served them." "And he built altars for all **the host of heaven** in the two courts of the house of the Lord. And he made his son pass through the fire, and observed times." Holy days were assigned to commemorate important celestial celebrities, the sun receiving preeminent attention.

In *Zephaniah 1:5* God's people are worshiping **the host of heaven** upon their housetops.

2 Kings 23:11 records how good king Josiah, as part of his reform policy, "took away the horses that the kings of Judah had given to **the sun**, at the entering in of the house of the Lord." And he "burned the **chariots of the sun** with fire." Ancient Persian, Greek, and Roman customs depicted the sun as a divine charioteer who daily drove his steeds across the sky.

Ezekiel 8:16 depicts a group of 25 men sitting in the temple doorway between the porch and altar with their backs turned toward the temple while their faces looked eastward. "And they **worshipped the sun** toward the east," an unspeakable abomination and insult to God.

Here the story of Nimrod deserves special inspection. *Josephus Antiquities Book 1 Chapter 4* describes Nimrod, the great grandson of Noah, as having "great strength." He was the driving force behind the tower of Babel project in defiance of God's promise to never again destroy the world by flood. This agrees with *Genesis 10:9,10* where Nimrod, "a mighty one in the earth" and "a mighty hunter before (against) the Lord," is said to have established the first kingdom on earth in Babel later extending it to Erech (or Uruk, named after the first city built before the flood, Enoch), Akkad, Nineveh and Calah—all in the land of Shinar or Sumer of archeological fame and today's Persian Gulf. He single-handedly built the original Babylonian Empire and distinguished himself as "the first man to rule the whole world." The *Encyclopedia Judaica* further indicates that he was "the first to eat meat and make war on other people." (Keter Publishing House Ltd., Jerusalem, Israel, 1971, vol. 12, p. 1167)

Jewish tradition also credits Nimrod with wearing the original animal skins that Adam and Eve were provided at their fall by the hand of God. At the pinnacle of his success, he inaugurated the practice of emperor-worship, leading the world of his time to "pay divine homage to him" as the one responsible for making the Sun to shine and life to spring from the earth. Extra-biblical accounts mention his order to kill all male children during the time of Abram's birth in a preview of Herod two millennia in advance. This animosity with "the Friend of God" later surfaces in the figure of Amraphel when he and three other buddies unknowingly cross the path of an adult Abraham.

Amraphel, according to the Talmud, is identified as Nimrod (cf *Targum Yonathan; Eruvin* 53a; Rashi) especially since he also is called the king of Shinar (Genesis 14:1). This would be theoretically possible, since his immediate contemporaries were reported to live over 400 years and he would have been only a little over 300 at the time of Lot's capture. Consider, for example, Salah (the grandson of Shem and second cousin to Nimrod) was also still alive during Abraham's lifetime.

Genesis 10 is a post-flood geneology which places Nimrod in relation to his contemporaries:

Noah

Shem

Arphaxad (born 2 years after the flood, lived a total of 456 yrs)

(53yrs) Salah (433 years total)

(30yrs) Eber

(34yrs) Peleg 104

(30yrs) Reu 136

(32yrs) Serug 166

(30yrs) Nahor 195

(29yrs) Terah 265

(70 yrs) Abram

Ham

Cush

Nimrod (only 265 years old at Abram's birth)

Japheth

If this is true, then Nimrod, now in his declining years and A.K.A. Amraphel, had the poor judgment of sacking Sodom and Gomorrah then leaving with Lot. When the news reached Abraham, he went into rescue mode, pursued after his abducted nephew and ultimately "slaughtered" the marauding kings in the valley of Shaveh at night in a four-prong attack with only 318 men (a strategy that Gideon would later employ against the Mideanites).

It is here that the legendary Semiramis enters the picture. Her name is the Hellenized form of Sumerian "*Sammur-amat,*" or "gift of the sea." Various historical references to this mysterious woman of antiquity tend to collaborate a common theme: she was a beautiful, shrewd and powerful ruler of ancient Sumer. Both famed as the wife and mother of Nimrod by different sources, the apparent conflict can be better understood when the entire story is considered.

Semiramis was originally Nimrod's wife, Queen of Shinar and ruler of a vast religious heirarchy of priests and priestesses. She was the real agent behind Nimrod's divine status which she strengthened even more after his death. While he was away on military exploits, she conceived an illegitimate son. Some accounts tell of Nimrod's return and threat to depose her; others that she arranged his death. But all agree that she explained the "miracle birth" as the result of an immaculate conception by Nimrod's returning spirit and that the newborn child was, in fact, Nimrod reincarnated.

The child was named *Damu*, or *Dammuzi* (in later Chaldean), and known as *Tammuz* in Hebrew, *Adonis* in Greek. Soon Tammuz became accepted as divine and became widely worshipped as the god of flocks and pastures, the heavenly shepherd. In many localities he was considered the god of springtime, raised to life again like his father Nimrod. As annual celebrations were established, the onset of summer heat and its withering effect of crops inspired the story that Tammuz was killed by a wild boar: spring had died. His death at the summer solstice was celebrated by national weeping and his name honored as the 4th month of the Babylonian calendar.

The custom of the Yule log also signified the death of Nimrod/Tammuz ("Yule" being the Chaldean word for "infant"). Cut down by his enemies and burned in a fire, he would reappear the following day as the splendid Christmas tree, risen from the ashes and triumphant.

Semiramis consequently deified herself as the mother of the god Damu (since only a god can beget a god), and installed herself as "The Queen of Heaven." She became the model for all subsequent goddesses, while Tammuz became the antitypical Father-Son figure adopted by every civilization since.

Jeremiah 44:18 reports the people of Israel burning "incense to **the queen of heaven**." She was Ishtar, the mother goddess of the Assyro-Babylonian culture. Cuneiform scripts from Mesopotamia describe her in the most remarkable flattery:

> 'I pray to thee, O Lady of ladies, goddess of goddesses…O gleaming one, Ishtar, assembler of the host…Where thou dost look, one who is dead lives; One who is sick rises up, the erring one who sees thy face goes aright…Faithfully look upon me and hear my supplication. Promise my forgiveness and let thy spirit be appeased.' Babylon, Albert Champdor, Eleck Books Ltd., 1958, p. 151

She was Ashtoreth, the goddess of fertility, maternity and sexual love in Palestine. In Ephesus she was the many-breasted Diana or Artemis. In Rome she was Venus, the goddess of love and death. In Asia she was Atargatis, the "Great Mother." She was the Italian Madonna, Belitini, "Our Lady," the morning and evening star.

The Queen of Heaven, a fitting title for the Sun King's widow, was also mother to Tammuz. This Mother-Son symbol is recognized in many cultures under numerous titles. Likewise, Nimrod/Tammuz, the Father-Son relationship is equally important. Both were diabolical corruptions of the original plan laid before the foundation of the world.

Christianity:	God the Father	Christ	Mary, Madonna
Hindu:	Brahma	Krishna	Queen of Heaven
India:		Iswara	Isi, Parvati
Egypt:	Seb	Horus/Osiris	Isis, Minerva
Rome:	Jove	Jupiter	Fortuna
		Bacchus	Mae Domina (My Lady)
Scandinavia:	Odin	Balder	Frigga
Ephesus			Diana
Greece:		Plutus	Ceres
		Adonis	Venus
			Ammas (ama “mother”)
Babylon:	Baal	Tammuz	Baalti
Assyria:	Bel	Nimrod	Semiramis

Apollo, “child of the sun,” is usually depicted with a halo, nimbus, solar disk or luminous circle enshrouding his head. Circe, “daughter of the Sun,” was illustrated in a Pompeii mosaic with the same halo. Hislop comments further on this nearly universal use of the sun disk.

> “Near the small town of Babain, in Upper Egypt, there still exists in a grotto, a representation of a sacrifice to the sun, where two priests are seen worshipping the sun’s immage… In the same temple of Babylon, the golden image of the Sun was exhibited for the worship of the Babylonians, In the temple of Cuzco, in Peru, the disk of the sun was fixed up in flaming gold upon the wall, that all who entered might bow down before it. The Pæonians of Thrace were sun-worshippers; and in their worship they adored an image of the sun in the form of a disk at the top of a long pole.” Hislop, *The Two Babylons*, p. 162.

In Arabia the moon is held in higher esteem than the sun as the supreme symbol of divinity. This is why the crescent moon is so widely employed in Arabian symbols, art, flags, and heraldry. According to their calendars, Lord Moon was born on the 24th of December. Elsewhere, as Plutarch recorded in his *De Iside,* vol. II, sec. 52, p. 372, the observance of sun worship at the end of the winter solstice (December 25) celebrated the appearance of “God incarnate.” This coincided with the “reappearance” of the sun which thereafter would begin to once again ascend higher in the sky as days became longer in length.

The Roman Catholic mass places special importance on the roundness of the eucharistic wafer-disk because it symbolizes the solar disk, emblem of the Son and Seed of the woman. Seeds were also depicted as a circle in ancient times. *Zer*, our Zero, was the term for seed. *Zero-ashta* "seed of the woman (Ashtarath)," became Zoroaster, head of the fire-worshipers. In the *Orphic Hymns* (Hymn xliv. 1) Bacchus (Zoroaster) is referred to as *Pyrisporus* (fire-born) *Pyr*—fire as in pyromaniac, *sporus*-born or seed as in spore.

Sadly, such is the legacy of this universal tradition.

Zodiac

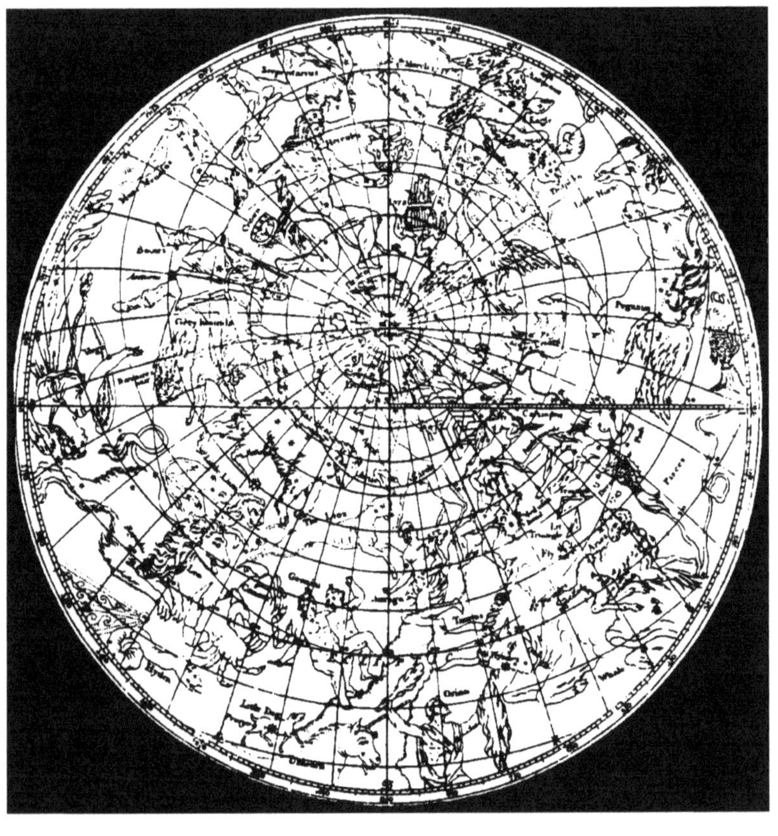
Serpentarius
Pegasus
Pisces
Auriga
Taurus
Hydra
Orion
Whale

Greek *zodiakos* means *A Circle,* derived from *Zoad* meaning *A Way, Path,* walking, stepping, as the lunar cycles (twelve in a year) mark the constellations each month. The zodiacal system is based on ecliptical coordinates.

The Twelve Signs of the Solar Zodiac

	The Suffering Saviour, delivery from the penalty of sin
1. **Virgo**	the Virgin and her Seed
2. **Libra**	the Scales, measuring the price to be paid
3. **Scorpio**	the Scorpion
4. **Sagittarius**	the Bowman aimed at the Scorpion
	The Glorified Blesser, delivery from the power of sin
5. **Capricornus**	the Dying Goat and Living Fish
6. **Aquarius**	the Waterman pouring out a flood across the sky
7. **Pisces**	the two Fishes
8. **Aries**	the Ram
	The Reigning Judge, delivery from the presence of sin
9. **Taurus**	the Bull
10. **Gemini**	the Twins or Couple
11. **Cancer**	the Crab: grasping and holding
12. **Leo**	the Lion leaping on Hydra, the Serpent

These signs trace the story of salvation from Genesis to Revelation. Virgo reminds us of the Seed of the Woman in *Genesis 3:15*; Leo represents the Lion of the tribe of Judah Who is ultimately victorious over the Dragon.

Each solar constellation has three associated minor constellations. These form **36 Decans**—directors—commented by Persians, Babylonians and Egyptians. Albumazar, the great Arabian astronomer of the middle ages (787-886) refers to "the Decans and their houses...which the Arabs in their language call faces. They are three to each sign of the Way." But he was by no means the first to mention them. Decans antedate Albumazar by nearly 3000 years. Decans appear in drawings inside coffin lids dated 2100 BC and Egyptian tomb ceilings including Ramses in Thebes.

The Egyptians identified Orion as Osiris, Sirius as a recumbent cow, Ursa Major as the front of a Bull. The most famous Egyptian star map is the first century BC stone found in the temple at Dandarah. Known as the Dandarah Zodiac, it now resides in the Louvre museum in Paris. By 1930 a definitive list of some 88 constellations were authorized by the International Astronomical Union.

The Lunar Zodiac

Oriental civilizations also described **28 Lunar Mansions**, the patch of stars surrounding the moon on each day of its monthly orbit. The Lunar Zodiac is thought to actually antedate the Solar version. In Arabia and India the Mansions of the Moon influenced numerous aspects of secular, political, literary, scientific and religious life. Children frequently are named in honor of the Mansions. Evidence of ancient knowledge also can be traced through Scandinavia, Burma, Mexico, Persia, and Spain.

☪ The 28 Lunar Mansions

Sign	Mansion	Meaning
Virgo	1 *Al Awa*	The Desired
	2 *Simak al Azel*	Branch of God's Power
	3 *Caphir*	The Atoning Sacrifice
Libra	4 *Al Zubena*	The Purchased Redemption
	5 *Al Iclil*	The Complete Submission
Scorpio	6 *Al Kalb*	The Wounding
	7 *Al Shaula*	The Deadly Wound
Sagittarius	8 *Al Naim*	The Gracious Delight
	9 *Al Beldah*	The Hasty Judgment
Capricorn	10 *Al Dibah*	The Slain Sacrifice
Aquarius	11 *Sa'ad al Bula*	Witness of the Rising
	12 *Sa'ad al Su'ud*	Witness of the Outpouring
	13 *Al Achbiya*	The Fountain of Pouring
Pisces	14 *Al Pherg al Muchaddem*	The Progeny of Ancient Times
	15 *Al Pherg al Muachher*	The Progeny of Latter Times
	16 *Al Risha*	The Joined Together
Aries	17 *Al Sheratan*	The Wounded and Cut Off
	18 *Al Botein*	The Treading Under Foot
	19 *Al Thuraiya*	The Punished Enemy
Taurus	20 *Al Debaran*	The Subduing Leader
	21 *Al Heka*	The Driving Away
Gemini	22 *Al Henah*	The Wounded Foot
	23 *Al Dirah*	The Ill-treated
Cancer	24 *Al Nethra*	The Treasured Possession
	25 *Al Terpha*	The Healing Deliverance
Leo	26 *Al Gieba*	The Exalted Prince
	27 *Al Zubra*	The Delayed Punishment
	28 *Al Serpha*	The Funeral-Pyre

The Twelve Signs and Their Decans

Virgo:	**Coma**, the Infant, the Branch, the Desired One
	Centaurus, a centaur with arrow piercing its victim
	Arcturus, the great Shepherd, Harvester, holding rod and sickle
Libra:	**Southern Cross**, under Centaur
	Centaur's Victim, slain, pierced to death
	Northern Crown, prized by the Serpent
Scorpio:	**Serpent**, struggling with Ophiuchus
	Ophiuchus, stung in one heel by the Scorpion,
crush-	ing it with the other
	Hercules, wounded heel, but foot over the Dragon's head
Sagittarius:	**Lyra**, a Lyre held by an eagle in triumph
	Ara, the burning Altar spilling its coals toward earth
	Draco, the Dragon coiled about the Pole
Capricorn:	**Sagitta**, the Arrow on its mission of death
	Aquila, the Eagle, pierced and falling
	Delphinus, the Dolphin leaping from the sea
Aquarius:	**Southern Fish**, drinking in the stream poured by Aquarius
	Pegasus, white winged horse, swiftly galloping with good tidings
	Cygnus, the Swan, bearing the sign of the cross
Pisces:	**Rod**, held by the Lamb, holding up the Fishes and holding down Cetus
	Cepheus, the great Victorious crowned King, standing on the polestar
	Andromeda, woman in chains, threatened by
Medusa's	cranial serpents
Aries:	**Cassiopeia**, the enthroned woman
	Cetus, the Sea-Monster, bound by the Lamb's rod
	Perseus, mighty warrior with winged feet, sword in hand, carrying the monster's head
Taurus:	**Orion**, the glorious Prince, sword on belt, his foot upon the Serpent's head
	Eridanus, Orion's tortuous River
	Auriga, the Shepherd carrying goats on his left arm, holding cords in his right hand

Gemini:	**Lepus**, the angry Serpent under Orion's feet **Sirius** (Canis Major), the Great Dog, the coming
Prince	
	Procyon (Canis Minor), the Second Dog following Sirius
Cancer: Pole	**Ursa Minor**, the Lesser Sheepfold, enclosing the
	Ursa Major, the Greater Sheepfold, near Arcturus, keeper of the flock **Argo**, the Ship, bearing the traveling Argonauts returning with the Golden Fleece
Leo:	**Hydra**, the fleeing Serpent, under Leo's foot **Crater**, the Cup of Wrath upon the Serpent **Corvus**, the Raven, bird of doom, tearing the Serpent

The Wanderers

Wandering stars, to whom is reserved the blackness of darkness forever. *Jude 13*

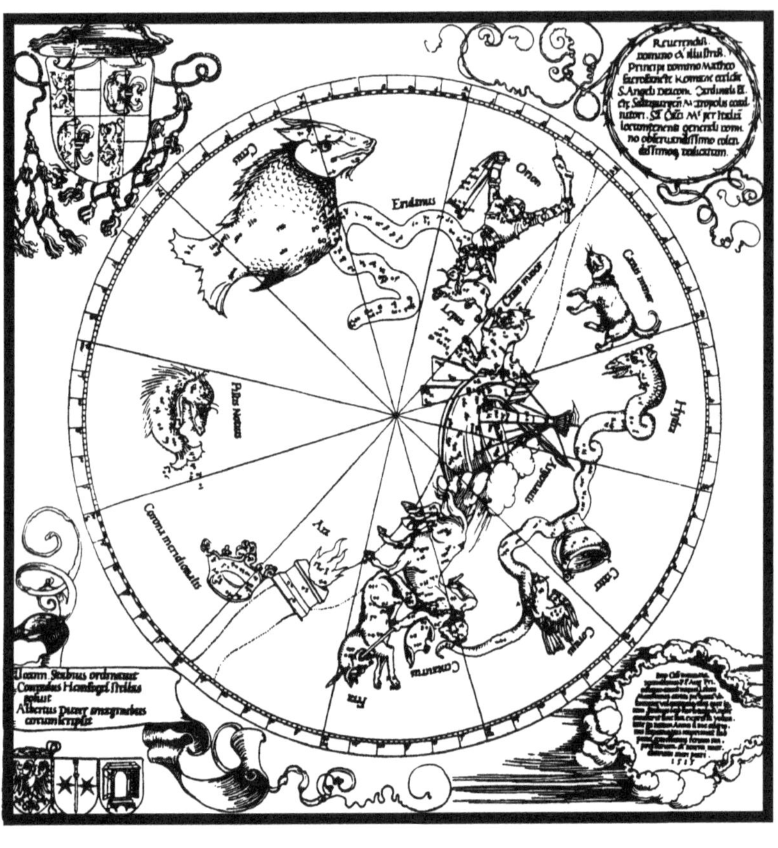

In addition to the *fixed* stars (fixed only in the relative sense that their apparent motion is infinitely slight), the ancients identified five wandering luminaries. Their movements could be traced over months to years in an erratic trail across the sky that would both advance and retreat. We now know the reason for this odd behavior. Planets within our solar system orbit along with the earth at different relative speeds causing their positions to constantly shift. These peculiar stars were named Mercury, Venus, Mars, Jupiter and Saturn. Adding in the Sun and Moon made a perfect seven, the most famous of all celestial bodies. Primitive peoples came to idolize these dynamic cosmic travelers as the seven great gods.

Job 41:1 refers to Leviathan as Cetus, the Sea-Monster.

"By His Spirit He hath garnished the heavens"
and by "His hand formed the fleeing Serpent."

Job 26:13

Job also speaks of *the crooked or fleeing Serpent* as evidence of God's greatness in forming the magnificent constellations. Is he alluding to Draco, or Hydra, or perhaps the Zodiac itself since it is often rendered as a serpent formed into a circle with its tail in its mouth? Hydra is probably the best choice as it is uniquely depicted in the act of escape.

Job, the book, is distinguished as the most original, most scientific, and the oldest literature in the Biblical canon. In fact, with a dating of about 2150 years BC, it precedes Homer by over a millennium and Thales, the earliest Greek philosopher, by some 1,500 years. Amazingly, the author of Job makes repeated astronomical references to named constellations.

Drummond records, "Origen tells us that it was asserted in the Book of Enoch (quoted by the apostle Jude) that in the time of that patriarch the constellations were already named and divided." Albumazer attributed the invention of the Zodiac to Hermes, named by Arab and Egyptian accounts as the patriarch Enoch. Josephus, the Jewish historian affirmed that the *starry lore* originated with the antediluvian patriarchs, Seth and Enoch.

Scripture tells us that God named the stars.

> "He calleth them all by their names." *Psalm 147:4*

> "Lift up your eyes on high and see who has created these stars, the One who leads their host by number, He calls them all by name." *Isaiah 40:26.*

Comparative linguistics has long been aware of the striking consistency among all language groups of similar word origins for the names of the weekly days. Even ancient languages—including Persian, Hindu, Chinese, Egyptian and Chaldean—name seven week days after the seven *planets,* as we continue to do even today:

Planets	**Babylonian**	**Roman**	**Italian**	**Saxon**	**English**
Sun	Shamash	Sol	Domenica	Sun	Sunday
Moon	Sin	Luna	Lunedi	Moon	Monday
Mars	Nergal	Mars	Martedi	Tuve	Tuesday
Mercury	Nabu	Mercurius	Mercoledi	Woden	Wednesday
Jupiter	Marduk	Jove	Giovedi	Thor	Thursday
Venus	Ishtar	Venus	Venerdi	Friga	Friday
Saturn	Nimurta	Saturnus	Sabato	Saturn	Saturday

Frances Rolleston, in her 1863 work *Mazzaroth,* traced the ancient meaning of star names. For example, Sirius, the brightest star in the sky is derived from an ancient root, *sur.* In other languages it retains its meaning of dignity and respect:

Egyptian	*osiris*	'a prince'
Hebrew	*sirai*	'a princess'
(Sarah's original name was Sarai)		
Etruscan	*aesar*	
Indian	*aswara*	
English	*sir*	

The word, Mazzaroth, is taken from *Job 38:32* where God asks Job, "Canst thou bring forth Mazzaroth in his season?" The word occurs in only one other scripture, *2 Kings 23:5* as Mazzaloth. It means, The Separated, The Divided, or The Apportioned and refers to the twelve signs of the solar zodiac which only God can bring forth in their season, one for each month of the year. Job also refers to the Pleiades in Taurus, the Chambers of the South in Scorpio, Orion, the Bear, and Hydra, the crooked serpent.

Rolleston's efforts were later popularized in the 1884 book, *The Gospel in the Stars* by J.A. Seiss, and shortly thereafter in E.W. Bullinger's *The Witness of the Stars* published in 1893.

Top 24 Magnitude Star Names and Meanings

Star	**Constellation**		
Sirius	Canis Major	Prince	Isaiah 9:6
Canopus	Argo	The Possession of Him Who Comes	Isaiah 60:4–9
Toliman	Centarus	The One Who Was and is to Come	Revelation 1:8
Vega	Lyra	He shall be Exalted	Isaiah 52:13
Capella	Auriga	She Goat	Ezekiel 37:22–24
Arcturus	Bootes	He Comes	Psalm 96:13
Rigel	Orion	The Foot That Crushes	Genesis 3:15
Procyon	Canis Major	The Reedemer	Isaiah 59:19,20; 49:24–26
Achemar	Eridanus	After Part of the River of Fire	2 Thess 1:7; Nahum 1:5
Altair	Aquila	The Wounded	Psalm 38:2,10; Isaiah 53:5
Agena	Centarus	…	

A-Crux	Southern Cross	…	
Betelgeuse	Orion	The Coming of the Branch	Isaiah 4:2; Malachi 3:1,2
Aldeberan	Taurus	The Governor	Psalm 22:28; Zech 9:7
Pollux	Gemini	He Who Comes to Suffer	1 Peter 1:11; Psalm 22
Spica	Virgo	The Branch	Zech 3:8; 6:12
Anates	Scorpio	Wounding	Isaiah 53:5; Zech 13:6
Fomalhaut	Pisces Australis	Mouth of the Fish	
Deneb	Cygnus	The Judge	Psalm 9:8
Regulus	Leo	Treading Underfoot	Isaiah 63:3; Genesis 3:15
B-Crux	Southern Cross	…	
Castor	Gemini	Ruler or Judge	Acts 7:27,35; Deut 18:15
Alioth	Ursa Major	Goat or Sin Offering	Leviticus 16:15,27
Bellatrix	Orion	Swiftly Destroying	Ezekiel 28:16

Virgo, The Woman and Her Seed

"There was a wonder in heaven, a woman standing on the moon, clothed with the sun"
Revelation 12:1

Virgo
Sagittarius
Aquila
Libra
Scorpio

God originally defined the constellations in a prophetic outline of salvation history. Each month features a different theme in the sequence of Redemption's Story. Although modern astrology begin their zodiacs with Aries (perhaps because it starts with 'A'?), the Biblical record points to the true starting point in the promised Seed of the Woman. Genesis chapter 3 features the very first scriptural prophecy. In a few powerful words, God reveals His plan to save fallen Man. He focuses on the Seed of the woman whose heel, though bruised by the cursed serpent, would crush the serpent's head.

This describes the cosmic picture of **Virgo**, the woman and her Seed. The Zodiac of Esne begins with this sign. In considering the story of redemption, this *is* the logical starting point. Virgo is a virgin.

The Greeks called her **Astrea, Athene**, or **Parthenos**, the maid of virgin goodness. The Hebrews called her **Bethulah**, the maiden. In Arabic she is **Adarah**, the pure virgin. In Egypt she is called **Aspolio**, *The Seed*.

But she is not only a virgin, she is a virgin *mother*. Hinduism teaches that Krishna, was divinely incarnated and born of a virgin. In Christianity the way of salvation is through Jesus Christ, the Son of God, *conceived by the Holy Ghost* and *born of a virgin*.

Ancient lore taught that the virgin would bring forth an illustrious *Seed*. Thus, Virgo is pictured as holding in her hand an ear of wheat, the *spica*. Indeed, the brightest star in the constellation is Spica. He who would come, to bruise the serpent's head, was to be *the seed of the woman*—a miracle birth, the only begotten Son of God.

> "Behold, a virgin shall conceive, and bear a son, and shall call His name Immanuel." *Isaiah 7:14; Matthew 1:23.*

When certain Greeks came to Philip to see Jesus, He applied the symbol of corn, a seed, that must fall, die and be buried in order to bring forth fruit. See *John 12:21–24.*

But in addition to holding the spica in one hand, Virgo holds a branch in the other. **Virgo**, Latin for *virgin,* is closely related to **Virga**, *a branch*. In Hebrew the word is *Tsemech.* Jesus is the "Rod from the stem of Jesse," the "Branch out of his roots" *Isaiah 11:1.* He is the "Branch of Righteousness," the "Branch of the Lord," and "God's servant the BRANCH" See *Isaiah 4:2, Jeremiah 23:5, Zechariah 3:8*. The Branch is a *Man* in *Zechariah 6:12*, and *God* in *Isaiah 4:2*. So likewise, each of the gospel writers display a distinct side of the Branch: Matthew presents Him as King, Mark shows Him as Servant, Luke as the Son of Man, and John as the Son of God.

The ancient names of the stars in this constellation reemphasize this theme of Branch and Seed as they apply directly to Christ:

Zavijava near Virgo's head...*Gloriously Beautiful*

> "In that day shall the branch of the Lord be beautiful and glorious." *Isaiah 4:2*

Vindemiatrix in Virgo's right arm...*The Son/Branch Who Comes*

Subilon in Virgo's right hand *Ear of Wheat*

> "I am the bread which came down from heaven." *John 6:41*

The First Decan: The Desired Coma

Known in modern charts as Coma Berenices (Bernice's Hair). Al Zimach (the shoot), Al Azal (the branch) and

Subilon (ear of wheat) speak of prophetic symbols. Albumazer (a Moslem Arab, and not a Christian) wrote:

> "There arises in the first Decan, as the Persians, Chaldeans, and Egyptians, and the two Hermes and Ascalillus teach, a young woman, whose Persian name denotes a pure virgin, sitting on a throne, nourishing an infant boy, said boy having a Hebrew name, by some nations call Ihesu, with the signification Ieza, which in Greek is called Christos." (*Latin translation in the British Museum, London*)

Even the celebrated Zodiac of Dendereh (which was brought to Paris by the French savants during the reign of Napoleon) pictured the Coma Decan of Virgo as a woman holding and admiring an infant. This first Decan of Virgo is called Coma which is derived from Hebrew and other Eastern sources meaning *desired* or *longed-for*. *Haggai 2:7* uses this root when speaking of Christ as *the Desire of all nations*. Egyptian astrology applied the term **Shes-nu**, the desired son, held on the lap of Isis and other goddesses. Shakespeare refers to *the good boy in Virgo's lap*.

"Unto us a Child is born; unto us a son is given."

Isaiah 9:6.

The Second Decan: The Despised Centaur

A vital and essential element of the Christian faith is the dual nature of the incarnate Christ. This 'mystery of Godliness' holds that our Redeemer became the God-Man, both the Son of God and the Son of Man, two natures in one Being, not by a conversion of Divinity into humanity, but by taking manhood into God. He is at once "the express image of [God's] person" and "the seed of Abraham." *Hebrews 1:3; 2:16*. He is Immanuel, God with us. "God was in Christ, reconciling the world unto Himself." *Matthew 1:23; II Corinthians 5:19*.

Centaurus captures the essence of Immanuel. Mythology presents these hybrid creatures (half man, half horse) as great bull-killers, born of the clouds, sons of God, but hated and abhorred by the gods and men, attacked and driven to the mountains and finally exterminated. Most striking is the account in classic mythology of the centaur Cheiron. Renowned for his skill in hunting, medicine, music, gymnastics and the art of prophecy, he was the friend of Hercules and the Argonauts on their voyage. Though he was immortal, he voluntarily agreed to die, transferring his immortality to Prometheus, and then allowing a poison arrow shot from heaven to strike himself, even though it was meant for another. God then raised him up and placed him among the stars.

Jesus, too, was a unique hybrid, combining two natures—wholly man and wholly God—in one being. As chief Centaur, He was Healer, Instructor, and Prophet. He fought the enemies of His friends. Yet, He, too, was despised and rejected of men. Though immortal himself, he chose to give up His life, that "whosoever believeth in Him should not perish but have everlasting life." *John 3:16.*

The name of this Decan in Arabic and Hebrew (*Bezeh*) means despised. *Cheiron,* a Greek word is derived from a Hebrew term meaning pierced. Herschel, the great English astronomer, observed that this star, the brightest in the constellation, is a type of variable star, ever changing in brilliance. Glorious at one time, dimmed and subdued at another, and then bright once more. Christ describes Himself in John's Revelation as the "One which is, and which was, and which is to come." Paul recounts the Messiah's experience in his letter to the Philipians: "Being in the form of God...took upon him the form of a servant and was made in the likeness of men...He humbled himself, and became obedient unto death, even the death of the cross. Wherefore God also has highly exalted him, and given him a name which is above every name." *Philippians. 2:6–9*

The Third Decan: Arcturus, the Shepherd

This stellar grouping has been given the name *Boötes* by the Greeks meaning the ploughman. *Bo* derives from Hebrew meaning the coming one. The Greeks also call this figure, *Arcturus,* the watcher, guardian or keeper of the Arktos or sheepfold. This would make *Arcturus,* the brightest star in the constellation, a shepherd. Another star, *Al Katurops,* is on the right arm of Boötes and means the Branch, the Rod or the shepherd's crook, the traditional symbol for the pastoral office.

Arcturus is clearly the Promised Seed of the Virgin, the "Good Shepherd that gives His life for the sheep." For "He shall feed His flock like a shepherd." "He is the chief Shepherd and Bishop of our souls." Did not Jesus say, "My sheep hear my voice, and I know them, and they follow me; and I give unto them eternal life; and they shall never perish, neither shall any man pluck them out of my hand?"

John 10:11, 27, 28; Isaiah 40:11; I Peter 2:25

Libra, Balancing the Scales

AN
IMV
S
INCVBVIT,
SVBIMAGINE
ALTIOR
MVNDI
Astrologia
ptolomeus

All eastern and most ancient Zodiacs include the figure of the scales. Among the Jews, this figure was represented by the last letter of the Hebrew alphabet, *Tau*. Very similar to our letter T, it takes the form of a cross, with a central pole supporting the balance beam. Being the final letter in the alphabet, it also signifies the end, the limiting boundary, termination and completion. When Jesus breathed His last upon Calvary's cross, He cried out, "It is finished."

This sign has received various names:

Hebrew	*Mozanaim*	the scales, weighing
Arabic	*Al Zubena*	purchase, redemption, gain
Coptic	*Lambadia*	station, house of redemption lam=graciousness; badia=branch
Greek	*Zugos*	horse or oxen drawn yoke crossbar, sandal's cross-strap, balance-beam

Stars within Libra have significant names, as well:

Zuben al Genubi	the price deficient
Zuben al Shemali	the price which covers
Al Gubi	heaped high
Zuben Akrabi	the price of conflict

Greek and Roman mythology associate this sign with Astrea or Athene, the patrons of justice, who still stand above government courts blindfolded and holding the balances aloft where the weight of evidence is tried, disputes are settled, and where the payment, penalty, and price of justice is measured out.

Balances suspended in the sky measure the plaintiff's indictments on one hand against the secured bond of his guarantor on the other. Libra's scales are tipped to say,

> "Thou are weighed in the balances, and art found wanting." *Daniel 5:27.*

The star marking the side raised high is *Zuben al Genubi,* "the price deficient." But the scale weighed down is found at *Zuben al Shemali,* "the price which covers."

The Southern Cross, the first Decan of Libra

Known as *crux,* the cross, this constellation is visible only by those living in the more southern latitudes, near or below the equator. Even there, the southern cross is located in the lowest part of the sky. Yet it is the most conspicuous star-group in the southern sky—distinct, separate and alone. Sailors have long depended on it to mark time at night. It is conveniently oriented in a true perpendicular upright position at midnight, being tilted to one side or the other while approaching and receding from the meridian.

The southern cross, as a named constellation, appeared for the first time in modern atlases in Royer's *Celestial Chart,* published in 1679. But Ulugh Beigh, Aben Ezra, and Albumazer (2, 4, and 8 centuries before Royer respectively) all name this south polar constellation as one of Libra's Decans. Because of the Earth's axial precession, this constellation has over time slipped steadily southward. Once as high as 16° above horizon in temperate northern latitudes, it has not been seen in northern skies for the past 2,000 years. Dante makes reference to it in his *Purgatorio* canto 1, translated by Carey:

> "To the right I turned, and fixed my mind
> On the other pole attentive, when I saw
> Four stars ne'er seen before save by the ken
> Of our first parents. Heaven of their rays
> Seemed joyous. O thou northern site! bereft
> Indeed, and widowed, since of these deprived!"

The cross consists of four bright stars and stands directly in the path of Virgo's second Decan, the dual-natured Seed of the woman. In Hebrew, *Adom,* it means cutting off. Gabriel advised Daniel that Messiah the Prince would be "cut off" from his people at a certain time. *Daniel 9:26*

This constellation is depicted in the Zodiac of Dendera by the figure of a lion, head turned back, mouth open and tongue hanging, the picture of an exhausted, thirsty beast. Christ, *the Lion of the tribe of Judah, knowing that all things were now accomplished, that the Scripture might be fulfilled, said,* "I thirst." One thousand years earlier, David by inspiration sensed the future experience of the coming Messiah and wrote: "I am poured out like water...My strength is dried up like a potsherd; and my tongue cleaves to my jaws." *Revelation 5:5; John 19:28; Psalm 22:14, 15.*

The ancient Egyptians illustrated a triad of three great gods, each holding the sacred Tau (cross) as the symbol of life and immortality. It is highly significant that the middle or second, known as the Conqueror and Deliverer, holds out the cross, extended to suggest a voluntary offering.

The Hindu Brahman deities also contain a divine triad. Here, too, the second is a son who is incarnated as a man-god. He is *Krishna,* the god of deliverance from danger and serpents. He sits cross-legged, holding the cross in his right hand and wears a cross on his chest. "It pleased the Father that in [Christ] should all fullness dwell; and, having made peace through the blood of His cross, by Him to reconcile all things unto Himself; by Him." *Colossians 1:19, 20*

Lupus, the Slain Victim: Libra's Second Decan

The next heavenly sign tells the story of the price paid on Calvary's cross. *Lupus,* the wolf of Greek and Latin accounts, is shown lying on its back, pierced by a barbed spear at the hand of Centaur himself. "The soul that sinneth, it shall die" *Ezekiel 18:20.* "Without shedding of blood is no remission [of sin]" *Hebrews 9:22.* Here we see the offering of life, the enduring agony of death. Jesus was made an offering for sin. He who knew no sin consented to be made a curse for us.

Ulugh Beigh identified this figure as *Sura,* a sheep or lamb. John's Apocalypse called Christ "the Lamb slain from the foundation of the world." *Revelation 13:8* Egyptians showed the victim as a naked, unresisting youth with a finger to his mouth. The Phoenicians named him *Harpocrates,* the god of quiet submission.

> "As a sheep before her shearers is dumb, so He openeth not His mouth." *Isaiah 53:7*
>
> Now once in the end of the world hath he appeared to put away sin by the sacrifice of Himself." *Hebrews 9:26*
>
> "Being found in fashion as a man, He humbled himself, and became obedient unto death, even the death of the cross." *Philippians 2:8*

Corona Borealis

This third Decan of Libra, is also called the Northern Crown. Greek mythology tells a tale of love behind the crown. It was supposedly a bridal gift from Bacchus to Ariadne who, because of her great love for Theseus, was killed at the hand of Artemis. But, because of her great beauty, was raised to a place among the immortals to wear her crown of stars. This is but a clumsy version of the original story. The Seed of the woman paid the price by his own life, because of His great love for mortals, to bring the object of His love out of the depths of depravity, to sit with Him in glory.

> "That at the name of Jesus every knee should bow,… and that every tongue should confess that Jesus Christ is Lord, to the glory of God the Father." *Philippians 2:10, 11*
>
> And "for the joy that was set before Him endured the cross, despising the shame." *Hebrews 12:2*

Scorpio

"Thou shalt tread upon the lion and adder; the young lion and the dragon shalt thou trample under feet." *Psalm 91:13*

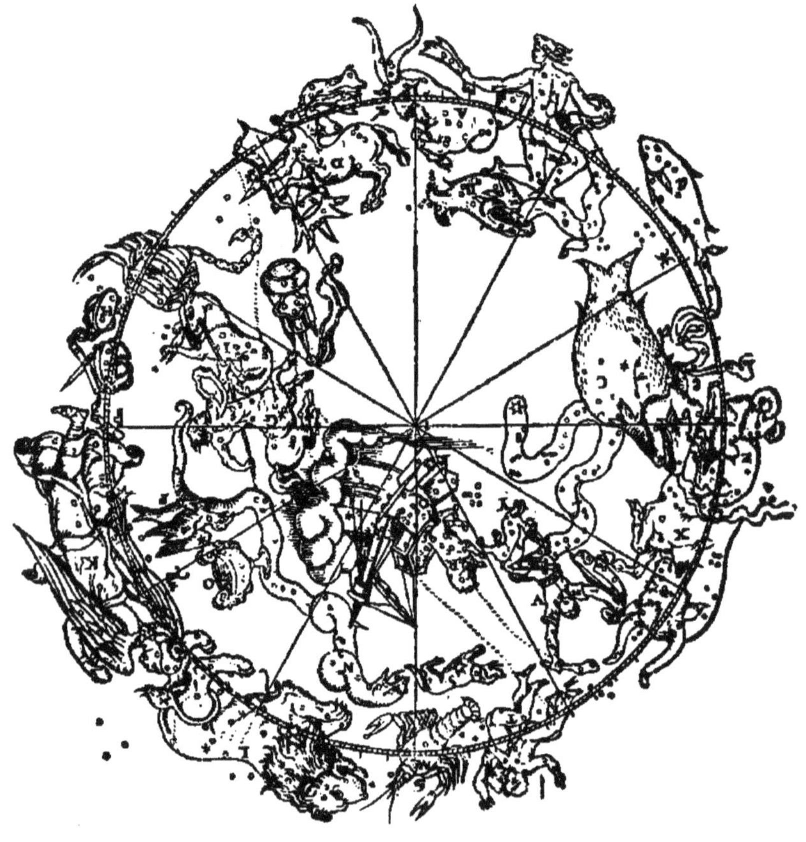

Jesus referred to this text in *Luke 10:19* when He said, "I give unto you power to tread on serpents and scorpions, and over all the power of the enemy." Our next sign shows a giant scorpion and dragon in conflict with a mighty warrior. *Al Akrab,* Arabic for scorpion, also means wounding, conflict. Coptic applies the term *Isidis,* attack of the enemy, oppression from deadly foes, and the principal star is *Antares,* cutting, tearing.

A lobster-like insect, the scorpion demands respect from his barbed tail, raised intent above its back charged with poisonous venom. The Egyptian version of this sign is a monster serpent, *Typhon* or Python, the hundred-headed father of Lernæan *Hydra,* the many-headed dog of Hell and *Chimæra,* his three-headed, fire-breathing sibling. The Hebrew Zodiac, that applied each of the twelve signs to the twelve tribes of Israel, identified this one as Dan who was, fittingly, described as "a serpent by the way, an adder in the path." *Genesis 49:17*

Scorpio attacks every chance it gets. As soon as the Seed of the woman was delivered, the Dragon stood ready to devour Him through Herod's army. As soon as He stepped from the waters of baptism onto Jordan's banks, the Devil was there to accost Him. A Nazareth mob tried to throw him from a cliff. As the climax of His mission drew near, the struggle intensified in Gethsemane. In agony Jesus wrestled with the powers of darkness. Into the heel of the divine Sufferer, the barbed tail thrust its deadly sting.

First Decan: Serpens, the Serpent

> "Hold that fast which thou hast, that no man take thy crown" was the admonition to Philadelphia. *Revelation 3:11.*

Python's jealous aim was to seize the crown. Serpens, in this Decan, is reaching out to do the same, and is only restrained by the strong arms of *Ophiuchus*. Just as *Spica* in Virgo is mirrored by the Infant in *Coma*, so the serpent in *Scorpio* is one and the same with Scorpio itself. Symbol of evil, and all that opposes God, who stands in the place of God, who says, "I will ascend into heaven," *Isaiah 14:13* this is that old serpent, the Devil, and Satan, who deceives the whole world, Apollyon, the Destroyer, the Accuser of the bretheren. *Revelation 9:11; I Cor. 10:10; Revelation 12:10.*

Ophiuchus, the Second Decan

"The Sun of Righteousness [shall] arise with healing in His wings." *Malachi 4:2* And when He came, He "went about all Galilee," "preaching the Gospel of the kingdom, and healing all manner of sickness and all manner of disease among the people." *Matthew 4:23*. Here we see the powerful arms of a man grasping the monstrous snake. Both hands grip the serpent, restraining it from the crown. One foot is lifted away, retreating from the scorpion's sting, while the other is crushing the scorpion's head. Krishna has been depicted in the same way in one Hindu pagoda.

Egyptian imagery often shows a man with an eagle or hawk's head. These birds of prey are notorious snake killers. The Greek term, Ophiuchus, originated from the Arabic *Cheleb Afei* or the Greek *Æsculapius*, honored by Socrates in his final hours. Æsculapius was a son of Apollo, the Sun god. His seven children (who personify his own qualities) were Healer, Physician, Desired One, Health-giver, Beautifier of good health, One who brings cures, and the Universal Remedy. Not only could he cure any patient, but he was also endowed with the power to raise the dead by virtue of the blood that ran from the side of the goddess Justice and the blood of the slain Gorgon (a monster of the underworld). Æsculapius was ultimately slain by a bolt of lightning from heaven because the god of hell complained of his good deeds. However, Apollo persuaded the other gods that he should be raised to glory.

This Greek myth is unmistakably taken from the constellation Serpentarius. Jesus is truly the Resurrection and the Life, the Universal Remedy, the true Sun of Righteousness. He died to silence the clamors of perdition, but by His marvelous merits, was raised and enthroned in the highest heavens.

Hercules, the Saviour

Last, we come to Hercules, the third Decan of Scorpio. The constellation shows him bent down on his right knee, holding a three-headed serpent in his left hand and holding in his right hand a large club raised high above his head. Five generations before the Greek Civilization, Phoenicians honored this figure in the sky as a savior. Though the Romans called him *Hercules*, the Greeks referred to this most famous of their legendary heroes as *Herakles*.

The mythical accounts portrayed him as the son of Zeus. But, being a man born of the gods, he was able to perform the most amazing feats, twelve in all:

> He almost effortlessly vanquished the Nemean lion released from Typhon and thereafter wore its skin.
>
> Next, he slew the nine-headed Hydra, captured the elusive golden-horned stag of Arcadia, and then the wild boar of Mt. Erymanthus.
>
> Next, he cleaned the stables of King Augeas in a single day, shot the swarms of giant Stymphalian birds, captured the mad bull of Crete, the man-eating mares of King Diomedes, and the girdle of Hippolyte, queen of the Amazons.
>
> At last, he seized the cattle of the triple-bodied giant Geryon, the Hesperidian apples from the end of the world, and (finally) the three-headed dog or snake that guarded the gates of hell.

It is this last foe which he holds in his celestial pose. Of course, Jesus was the real God-Man. He faces head-on the Devil, "who goes about as a roaring lion, seeking whom he may devour." Michael fought the Dragon, the war was in heaven. He prevailed against the principalities and powers of darkness and made a display of them. The cattle on a thousand hills are His. *I Peter 5:8; Revelation 12:7; Psalm 50:10.*

Sagittarius, The Archer

"In Thy majesty ride prosperously, because of truth and meekness and righteousness; and Thy right hand shall teach Thee terrible things. Thine arrows are sharp in the heart of the King's enemies." *Psalm 45:4, 5*

What contrasts there are concerning the Messiah. Though He would not bruise a reed, he would bring a sword. His yoke was easy and His burden was light; but narrow and straight was the way He led. He was meek and lowly in heart, yet He comes terrible as an army with banners. He comes to bring vengeance on His enemies, riding on a white horse holding a bow. King of kings and Lord of lords, He goes forth "conquering and to conquer." He leads the charge against injustice with invincible and terrible majesty. *Revelation 19:11; 6:2; Revelation 19:16*

All constellation charts name this mighty One, the Archer or the Bowman. The Greeks called Him *Cheiron,* the noble chief centaur, executing justice. In his starry stance, he aims his arrow at the Scorpion's heart. Jesus came to destroy the works of the Devil. But at the same time He says, "I delight to do Thy will, O my God: yea, Thy law is within my heart. I have preached righteousness in the great congregation." *Psalm 40:8,9.* And, on horseback, He comes quickly. "Behold, I come quickly; and my reward is with me." *Revelation 3:11.* "The great day of the Lord hasteth greatly." *Zephaniah 1:14.*

Lyra, the Harp, is Decan One

Psalm 21 describes the Almighty shooting His arrows against His enemies: His right hand shall find them out, and His wrath shall swallow them up. Their fruit shall be destroyed from the earth, and their seed from among the children of men. Then there is rejoicing and singing, a new song, the song of Moses and the Lamb, and the 144,000 stand on the sea of glass with harps in their hands. *Revelation 14:1–3*

The harp is the oldest of stringed instruments. It was named along with the shepherd's pipe 300 years before Adam died (*Genesis 4:21*). Greek legend names Orpheus as the most renowned of harpists. And his harp has become the symbol of joy and delight and praise. So magnificent his music, that rivers forgot to flow, wild beasts were tamed, trees from Olympic forests moved near to hear him play, and sufferers lost their pain.

This is when the morning stars sang for joy, when the 24 elders sang to the Lamb: Glory and honor and wisdom and power and blessing... When the seraphim and cherubim covered their faces with their wings and sang, "Holy, Holy, Holy." And every creature in heaven, and on earth, and under the earth, and upon the sea, and all things sang out, "To Him that sits upon the throne and to the Lamb, be the blessing, and the honor, and the glory, and dominion for ever and ever." This is the jubilant gladness of Orpheus. The brightest star in the northern sky was not picked by coincidence to bejewel the harp. This star is Vega, the triumphant warrior, the exalted Victor over Death and Hades. *Job 28:7; Revelation 5:13; 4:8; 1:6*

Some constellation charts show this Decan as an eagle, the natural enemy of snakes, holding the harp or flying behind it.

Ara, the Altar

The Arabs called this second Decan, *Al Mugamira,* the completion, the finish, the end. Greeks called it *Ara,* an altar or funeral-pile. It was also the name of the goddess of revenge and destruction. In Hebrew it is *mara* or aram, which means a curse, utter destruction.

Originally, these constellations appeared in the lowest portion of the southern sky. The regions beyond were considered to be the underworld or lower regions, the regions of darkness. The altar flames of this constellation are pointed downward toward the invisible perdition of the south pole and the lake of fire.

"Now is come salvation and strength, and the kingdom of our God, and the power of His Christ: for the accuser of our brethren is cast down." A mighty angel bound the Devil and cast him into the abyss and then into the lake of fire and brimstone. *Revelation 12:10; 20:1–3, 10*

Draco, The Dragon Decon Number Three

The dragon symbolizes danger, evil, terror, cunning, artifice, deceit, defiant power and devastating force. Terrific, oppressor, assailing with teeth and claws, armed with spines and spiked tail, fire-breathing fury that flies on great wings. Persecuting tyrant, the Dragon is very popular in oriental art, and a common theme of classic Greek and Roman literature. All cultures know of this horrid creature and have incorporated the concept in their religions, heraldry, art and literature.

The Dragon's constellation coils around nearly one-half of the entire northern sky, his tail alone sweeping over "the third part of the stars." John saw a great portent in heaven, a great red Dragon, having seven heads and ten horns and upon his heads seven crowns. His tail drew a third of the stars of heaven. He stood before the woman ready to devour her child as soon as it was born. But the child escaped and was caught up to heaven. Then there was war in heaven and the great dragon was thrown down along with his angels to the earth. The dragon chased the woman into the wilderness and made war with her descendants. But he is finally destroyed by the Lord of lords and King of kings as he returns with the hosts of heaven. *Rev. 12:2–17; 19:11–20.*

> "God is my King of old, working salvation in the midst of the earth.... Thou breakest the heads of the dragons in the waters. Thou Breakest the heads of leviathan in pieces." *Psalm 74:12–14.*

> "In that day the Lord with His sore and great and strong sword shall punish Leviathan the crossing serpent, even Leviathan that crooked serpent; and He shall slay the Dragon." *Isaiah 27:1*

The brightest star in this constellation has several telling names:

Al Waid, who is to be destroyed
Thuban, the subtle
Al Dib, the reptile

The second most dominant star is *Rastaban,* head of the subtle.

The third is *Etanin,* the long serpent, the Dragon.

Other stars include:

Grumian, the deceiver
El Athik, the fraud
El Asieh, the humbled, brought down
Gianser, the punished enemy

Astronomical Evangelism, Evangelic Astronomy

The Solar Zodiac can be divided into three groups of four constellations:

The first group deals with the Redeemer—His Person, Work, and ultimate Triumph

Virgo, the virgin who delivered the Man child, the promised Seed
Libra, the cross of divine justice where the merits of our Saviour tipped the balance
Scorpio, the enemy who wounds His heel
Sagittarius, the coming King who wounds the Dragon's head

The second group centers on the Fruits of His Work and Mediation—the Church

The third and final group features the final united glory of the Redeemed with their Redeemer

Now, we focus on the second group of constellations dealing with the "remnant of her seed, which keep the commandments of God and have the testimony of Jesus Christ *Revelation 12:17.*" This is spiritual Israel, born out of the sacrificial death of Christ. He dies that they might live. His death is their birth. Like the phoenix arising out of the ashes of its consumed predecessor, we see in the first sign of the middle group the same lesson.

Capricorn, the hybrid Goat-Fish

The goat was a sacrificial animal, used by ancient Israel as a sin-offering. *Leviticus 9:3*. Aaron "took the goat, which was the sin-offering for the people, and slew it, and offered it for sin...God hath given it you to bear the iniquity of the congregation, to make atonement for them before the Lord." *Leviticus 9:15; 10:17.*

The starry figure of Capricorn is shown in a dying position, one leg folded under, the other extended but unable to lift him up. His head is falling, sinking in a final agonal nod. "When Jesus therefore had received the vinegar, He said, It is finished: and He bowed His head, and gave up the Ghost." *John 19:30.* This is a picture of God's sacrifice, "wounded for our transgressions," "bruised for our iniquities." *Isaiah 53:5.* The most prominent stars in Capricorn are *Gedi* and *Dabih*, which means cut-off, hewn-down, slain.

But the goat is also a fish, another kind of life forming out of this sacrificial death and vitally connected with it. Jesus reminds us that we branches must be connected with the vine to survive. *John 15:5.* And here we see a living fish and a dying goat. Jesus said, "I will make you fishers of men." *Matthew 4:19*. But the idea was not new. Long before

God told the children of Israel that He would bring them back to their own land: "I will send for many fishers, and they shall fish them." *Jeremiah 16:16*. Ezekiel saw the same vision of water gushing forth across the land. "And there shall be a very great multitude of fish, because these waters shall come thither." *Ezekiel 47:9*

When Jesus spoke with Nicodemus, He said that those who would have eternal life must be "born of water." *John 3:5*. He even taught this idea in the parable of the net: "The kingdom of heaven is like unto a net, that was cast into the sea, and gathered of every kind." *Matthew 13:47*

The Greek word for fish, *Icthus*, was used by the early Christian church as an acronym for

Ie*s*us	Jesus
cristos	Christ
theos	God
soteron	Saviour

Jesus is the divine Fish, who in the waters of baptism bears a congregation of fishes. He is at once the sacrificial goat, the sin-offering, the Head of the flock and the Progenitor of His Church, the saved of all ages, reborn men and women, who live because of Him.

Half goat, half fish. This is a symbol that has no counterpart in nature. It is above nature. It is supernatural, miraculous. So, too, the hybrid symbol of Christ, Himself: half horse, half man. He is the Son of God; He is the Son of Man. He is the God-Man. "And without controversy great is the mystery of godliness: God was manifest in the flesh." *1 Timothy 3:16*

The Goat and Fish are also one, one body, a mystical union. Jesus is the head, we are the members. He is the Vine we are the branches. He is the Christ, we are Christians. Incorporated in Him, and He in us. This is "the mystery which hath been hid from ages and from generations, but now is made manifest to his saints: to whom God would make known what is the riches of the glory of this mystery among the Gentiles; which is Christ *in* you, the hope of glory." *Colossians 1:26, 27*

The theme has various corruptions in ancient cultural myths. Greek legend tells the story in a more absurd way: The gods were feasting together near a river when the terrible *Typhon* appeared. They all assumed other shapes and forms to escape his fury. Pan or Bacchus took the form of a goat and plunged into the river. The part of his body submerged below the water took on the form of a fish.

This is exactly what Jesus did for us. To secure deliverance from the Devil's threats, Jesus took upon Himself the form of a Sin-bearing sacrificial goat and plunged into the waters of death, sinking in sin as our substitute so that we might become a living part of Him, never more to be separated from Him.

Counterfeits on this theme occurred in the half-man half-fish god of the Philistines, *Dagon* and of the Babylonians, *Oannes*.

Sagitta, the Arrow

Appearing alone, in flight, speeding toward its target, the Arrow is shot by an invisible archer from heaven. It comes from the throne of Almighty Justice, directed at an unrighteous world, but instead strikes the spotless, guiltless Son of God who falls as a stricken goat. *Psalm 38* describes the wounded Sufferer.

Aquila, the wounded Eagle

Aquila is pierced, falling and dying just like the grain of wheat falling and dying. The dominant star is of first magnitude named, *Al Tair*, "the wounded." The second star means "covered with blood." And the third is "torn." Yet another means "wounded in the heel." Christ said to the children of Israel, "I bare you on eagles' wings and brought you unto myself." *Exodus 19:4*. Moses reminded his people of this shortly before his death, "As an eagle stirreth up her nest, fluttereth over her young, spreadeth abroad her wings, taketh them, beareth them on her wings; so the Lord alone did lead him." *Deuteronomy 32:11,12*

The eagle is the serpent's enemy as depicted on the Mexican flag. As the King of birds, the eagle is a noble, royal bird.

The Dolphin Decan

Dolphinus depicts a fish leaping out of the water, springing forth, vibrant life out of the depths of death. It repeats the same idea as the dying goat transforming into a living fish. Jesus not only died for our sins, but rose again to become "the first-fruits of them that slept." *I Corinthians 15:20* "Like as Christ was raised up from the dead, by the glory of the Father, even so we also should walk in newness of life." *Romans 6:4*. Resurrection to a new life.

Greek mythology positioned the dolphin as sacred to Apollo who assumed its form when he showed the Cretan colonists the way to Delphi. Jesus took on our form in order to save us from the Dragon's power. "In all things it behooved Him to be made like unto His brethren, that He might be a merciful and faithful high priest to make reconciliation for the sins of the people." *Hebrews 2:17*

Capricorn summarizes the truths of the gospel: the goatfish dying in its head, but living still in its feet; falling as an eagle pierced and wounded by the arrow of death, but springing up from the dark waves as a vigorous dolphin.

Aquarius, The Water-Bearer

With a giant bowl (situla) hefted up and pouring out its precious contents, Aquarius sends a stream of water that becomes a river (*fluvius aquarii*) flowing across the heavens. The Greeks called him *Ganymedes*, the bright, glorified youth, so beautiful, beloved, and favored that the King of the gods carried him to heaven on eagle's wings to live among the immortals. But this is clearly referring to "the chiefest among ten thousand, and altogether lovely." *Song of Solomon 5:10,16* He is the One who said, "I will pour water upon him that is thirsty, and floods upon the dry ground: I will pour my Spirit upon thy seed, and my blessing upon thine offspring;" *Isaiah 44:3*. "I will pour out my Spirit upon all flesh; and your sons and your daughters shall prophesy, your old men shall dream dreams, your young men shall see visions." *Joel 2:28*

Water is the undeniable essence of life. Our bodies are over 70% water by weight. Pure water quenches the thirst of man and beast and land. Both delicate mist and pelting rain make the barren soil a verdant garden. The righteous man is described as "a tree planted beside the rivers of waters." *Psalm 1:13*. God speaking through Moses said, "My doctrine shall drop as the rain, my speech shall distill as the dew, as the small rain upon the tender herb, and as the showers upon the grass." *Deuteronomy 32:2*. Jesus was foretold by Zechariah to be "as a fountain opened to the house of David, and to the inhabitants of Jerusalem, for sin and for uncleanness." Ezekiel described the blessing of the gospel as water gushing forth from the sanctuary ever rising until, no longer able to stand, those immersed in it must swim. *Ezekiel 47:1–6*. Jesus, speaking to the woman at the well, said that His Word would be to her as a fountain of water springing up unto everlasting life. And those who drink from it, would never thirst again. *John 4:14*

The brightest star in the constellation is *Sa'ad al Melik,* Record of the outpouring. Water is a symbol of the Spirit. In the beginning, the Spirit of God brooded over the face of the waters. *Genesis 1:2.* The Spirit has always been in the world, but He was "poured out" in greater measure, as promised, *Acts 2:1–4* on the day of Pentecost. "The early and the latter rains" *Joel 2:23* in abundance are promised to mature the harvest. Moses was instructed to smite the Rock, a symbol of Christ who would be smitten for us, and out of it would gush forth a miraculous river of water. As fishes, the people of God thrive in the water of life. *Revelation 22:1.* And in the holy city, the new Jerusalem a river of life flows from the throne of God. *Revelation 22:1.* So Jesus invites all: "If any man thirst, let him come unto Me, and drink." *John 7:37.* "HO everyone that thirsteth,... let him to the waters... come and buy wine without money and without price." *Isaiah 55:1*

Piscis Australis, the Southern Fish

The first Decan is yet another fish, responding to the Saviour's invitation and drinking in the stream flowing from Aquarius' bowl.

Mythology attributes this fish to Astarte (Aphrodite by the Greeks, Venus by the Romans) who appears as a fish in order to escape (as Bacchus-Pan did) from the horrible Typhon. So we are admonished: "Be not conformed to this world: but be ye transformed by the renewing of your mind." *Romans 12:2.* Astarte was the moon goddess and representing motherhood in general. Joseph interpreted the moon in his vision as his mother. *Genesis 37. Revelation 12:1* uses a woman standing on the moon as the symbol of God's church, the bride of Christ, the mother of the saints. *Galations 4:26.* This too is the symbol of marriage, union of man and wife, so that the two become one. This is the union between Christ and His church.

Pegasus

The second Decan is a flying horse. The Greek name means "horse of the gushing fountain." This celestial horse is the favorite of the Muses. Standing upon Mount Helicon, its hoofs astride the Pierian springs. It was born as Perseus beheaded Medusa, lived in the palace of Jupiter, king of the gods. Belerophon obtained him after sacrificing to the goddess of justice and receiving the golden bridle. With it, Belerophon was able to control the wild and winged stallion, enabling him to slay the Chimaeran monster. In the process, however, he receives a painful sting on his foot.

Zechariah tells of four wild horses sent by God "to walk to and fro through the earth." *Zechariah 6:5–7*. Their mission was to restore liberty, peace, and blessing to God's people. Pegasus moves with heavenly speed. '*Pega*' (also rendered 'Peka' or 'Pacha') means *chief*. The last part of his name, '*sus*' means a swiftly returning horse. Other stars in the constellation include *Markab* 'the returning', *Scheat* 'he who goes and returns', *Enif* 'the branch', *Al Genib* 'he who carries', *Homan* 'the waters', and *Matar* 'he who causes the overflow'.

The gospel, the good news, was to be preached into all the world. *Matthew 24:14; 28:20; Revelation 6:2*. This was the commission. The true Pegasus was the newborn church, herald of salvation to the Gentile world: Romans, Greeks, Egyptians, Asians, Medes, Cretes and Arabians. No barriers could keep the winged horse from taking the message around the world.

Cygnus, the swan

Eighty-one stars embracing five double stars and one quadruple, one binary, 61 Cygni, is one of our closest stars. In addition to co-orbiting each other, the pair are traveling at an enormous speed to some other destination. The constellation forms the figure of a swan, king of water birds, the emblem of dignity, purity, and grace in flight. The Greek and Latin forms of the name mean "circling and returning."

It is flying in the same direction as the river flowing from Aquarius' urn. With its long extended neck and outstretched wings, the stars form a large cross.

It's stars are named:

Deneb	"the Lord or Judge to come"
Azel	"who goes and returns"
Fafage	"glorious, shining forth"
Sadr	"who returns as in a circle"
Adige	"flying swiftly"
Arided	"He shall come down"

Several stories emerge from classical mythology that hint at the original concept of the swan. One account involves the son of Apollo, who while hunting jumped into Lake Canope and was transformed into a swan. Another tells of Poseidon's son when strangled by Achilles (because he could not be harmed by iron) turned into a swan and flew away. Yet a third concerns the son of Athenelus who was destroyed by Jupiter for his poor handling of the chariot of the sun. When his friend bereaved his fate, Apollo changed him into a swan and placed him among the stars.

All three tales describe a son of the gods. Christ is the Son of God. As such He is immortal and invincible. However, he volunteered His life to save those who would be destroyed. *John 10:18*. But He rose again, transformed into a new and glorious body, raised and exalted on high to sit once again on His Father's throne in heaven. *Hebrews 1:3*. He extends His glorious arms, no longer outstretched upon a cross, but because of Calvary, now able to "save to the uttermost them that come unto God by Him." *Hebrews 7:26*. And he cries out to all who will listen, "If any man thirst, let him come unto Me, and drink." *John 7:37* "Ho, everyone that thirsteth, come ye to the waters, and he that hath no money, come ye, buy, and eat; yea, come, buy wine and milk without money and without price." *Isaiah 55:1* "And the Spirit and the Bride say, Come....and let him that is athirst come. And whosoever will, let him take the water of life freely." *Revelation 22:17*

Take the water and drink deep, drink earnestly, with all the fullness of your soul. For "whosoever drinketh of the water that I shall give him shall never thirst; but the water that I shall give him shall be in him a well of water springing up into everlasting life." *John 4:14*

The Fishes

Jesus, watching Peter and his brother, Andrew, casting their nets into the sea, called out to them, "Follow me, and I will make you fishers of men." *Matthew 4:19*. I will teach you how to cast your net into the world, and haul in a multitude of souls. Later He would teach them a parable of this same truth: "The kingdom of heaven is like unto a net that was cast into the sea, and gathered of every kind [of fish]. Which when it was full, they drew to shore, and sat down, and gathered the good into vessels, but cast the bad away." *Matthew 13:47, 48*. Jesus made fish the symbol of His Church.

The new life that Christ promises, arises in the form of a fish from the dying body of a sacrificial goat. Those coming to drink in the stream poured by the heavenly Waterman are pictured as a great leaping fish. Now we examine the sign of the fish.

Pisces

Today, this sign is listed first in the Zodiac. Originally, it was seventh. It is, in fact, two fishes, one swimming north toward the pole star, the other parallel to the sun's path. Though they are separated, they are tied by two long bands to the foot of the Ram.

In Syriac the name is *Nuno,* "the Fish prolonged, prosperous." In Coptic the name is *Picot Orion,* "the Fish congregation of the coming Prince." Two dominant stars are *Okda,* "the united," and *Al Samaca,* "the upheld."

Mythology tells of Venus and Cupid being surprised one day while they were on the banks of the river Euphrates by the sudden appearance of Typhon, the giant monster. As so many others have done, they plunged into the water, changed themselves into fishes and swam away to safety. Venus was believed to be hatched from an egg laid by a heavenly dove. Cupid was supposedly the firstborn of the created world and aided in some way with the world's original creation. So, too, Christ is "the firstborn of every creature" *Colossians 1:15.*

Two fishes would indicate two churches. Zechariah saw a vision of two olive trees. *Zechariah 4:3.* Paul used the same image in speaking about the Gentile church as grafted onto the original olive tree. *Romans 11:17.* The Church of the Patriarchs gave birth to the Church of Christ. *Acts 7:38.* Stephen refers to the church in the wilderness. Paul, in the book of Hebrews points out in chapter 11 that the saints from Adam onward could not be made perfect without us, the saints of the New Testament dispensation. The two churches are bound together and dependent on each other.

So in the picture of the first Decan, *the Band.* The two fish are tied together by two ribbons of stars. They are caught, not free to swim their own course, but held by the hand of the Lamb. They are His, governed by His power, His will,

His grace. "Without Me ye can do nothing." *John 15:5*. But "Fear thou not, for I am with thee; be not dismayed; for I am thy God: I will strengthen thee; yea, I will help thee; yea, I will uphold thee with the right hand of my righteousness." *Isaiah 41:10*

Cepheus

Sitting nearby on his throne is the protector of the Fishes. Clad in royal robes, crowned and holding high his scepter he sits in noble bower with one foot on the Pole star. The bright star that marks his right shoulder is *Al Deramin*, "the Quickly Returning One." In the figure's girdle shines *Al Phirk*, "the Redeemer." The left knee contains another star known as "the Shepherd."

The Egyptians called him *Pe-ku-hor*, the Coming Ruler. *Cepheus* means the King, the royal Branch. *Zechariah 6:13* records that the Branch "shall bear the glory, and shall sit and rule upon His throne." Paul recounts that even though Jesus was made "a little lower than the angels for the suffering of death," *Hebrews 2:9* and having "humbled himself," *Philippians 2:9* to the cross for our redemption, "God also hath highly exalted Him," "and set Him on His own right hand in the heavens, far above all principality, and power, and might, and dominion, and every name that is named, not only in this world, but also in that which is to come, and put all things under His feet." *Ephesians 1:19–22*

Andromeda

Shackled by chains, restrained and unable to rise, the beautiful woman of Andromeda is also a symbol of God's church. *Andro-medo* is Greek for "man-ruler." The church will indeed rule over men. When Peter inquired as to what possible compensation he and his fellow supporters might expect for having sacrificed jobs and reputation to follow the Messiah, Jesus promised them that "when the Son of man shall sit in the throne of His glory, ye also shall sit upon twelve thrones, judging the twelve tribes of Israel." *Matthew 19:28*. Paul later confirmed the same idea when he wrote the Corinthians. "Do ye not know that the saints shall judge the world?" *1 Corinthians 6:2* And John observes that in the end, the saved of heaven would forever praise Christ because He "has made us kings and priests unto God." *Revelation 1:6.*

In Genesis Adam was granted dominion over the world. In Revelation the Second Adam grants dominion to those whom He redeems.

But the chains leave the woman, the Church, bound hand and foot. The names of the prominent stars in this Decan echo this thought: the broken-down, the weak, the afflicted, the chained. Greek mythology tells the story of Andromeda as the daughter of Cephus and Cassiopeia. She was betrothed to her uncle Phineus, but the promised wedding was spoiled when Neptune (at the request of his favorite nymphs, Juno and Nereides) sent a flood complete with sea-monster to crash the event. The nymphs were retaliating because Cassiopeia had claimed to be more beautiful. Neptune's fury was relentless until Jupiter finally insisted that Andromeda be chained to a rock near the Joppa shoreline as an offering to the sea-monster. Luckily, Perseus happened to be returning from his victory over the Gorgons and rescued her in the nick of time. She was so grateful, she accepted his marriage proposal and became his bride and wife.

The story is captivating in its parallel to the woman of *Revelation 12*. The common themes of jealousy, persecution, and intent to kill an innocent victim are unmistakable. The woman is pictured with a dragon standing before her, ready to devour her newborn child. She is pursued into the wilderness, hunted by her angry assailant.

History bears the truth of Revelation's prophetic account. Captured and tortured since the time of Saul, tormented by Roman persecution (pagan and papal), the church has persevered through Waldensean strongholds and into New World exiles, suffering under European monarchies and communist oppression, revolutionary suppression and evolutionary denial. But the time will come when the bonds will be broken, the ordeal will end. The Lord of lords and King of kings is coming, *Canticles 6:4,10* as "terrible as an army with banners," to rescue the captive maiden from certain doom and make her His glorious bride, "free of spot and wrinkle." *Ephesians 5:27.*

Pisces, from ancient times, has been held as an ominous sign, filled with superstitious bodings of violence and death. So much was this sign abhorred, that the Syrians and Egyptians widely abstained from eating fish. In fact, the Egyptian hieroglyphics symbolized fish for the concept of hatred, "sounds fishy." This is the general regard which persists today of the world in general for the purpose, claims, and teachings of God's church. His invitations to purity and holiness, to love and kindness, to gentle sympathy and to self-sacrificing consideration for His other children, is offensive, distasteful, and repulsive to the hedonistic, self-centered orientation of many who live only for the "good life," "what's in it for me," and "let's party."

Aries, The Ram

The last of the four signs relating especially to the Church is a ram. The Lamb of God, the prince of the flock, and at the same time, our High Priest, and Blessed Hope. "Worthy is the Lamb that was slain to receive power, and riches, and wisdom, and strength, and honor, and glory, and blessing." *Revelation 5:12*. The song of triumph rings out when the Lamb that was slain returns as the Shepherd-King descending Himself "from heaven with a shout, with the voice of the archangel, and with the trump of God." The returning Lamb shouts "and the dead in Christ shall rise first: then we which are alive and remain shall be caught up together with them in the clouds, to meet the Lord in the air." *I Thessalonians 4:16, 17*

Aries (Chief, Head) comes from *Aryan* meaning Lordly. Christ is the head of the Church. Even the English term *Ram* signifies "elevated, lifted up." The Arabic name *Al Hamal* is translated "The Gentle Sheep." Principal stars in this constellation are:

El Nath (Natik)	"The Wounded or Bruised"
Al Sharetan	"The Slain"

Above the head of Aries is a triangle of stars which Greek astronomers identified as a sign of the Trinity.

Here is "the Lamb of God, which taketh away the sin of the world" *John 1:29* by His sacrifice for mankind. But He is also "the Lamb in the midst of the throne." This is the Lamb to Whose Marriage Supper the world is invited. This is the Lamb Who alone is worthy to break the seals and complete the mystery of God. This is the Lamb Whose blood enables us to overcome the dreaded beast. This is the Lamb Who fills the New Jerusalem with light eternal. *Revelation 5:6, 19:9, 5:5, 12:11, 21:23.*

Mythology records the story of Aries, a mysterious animal presented as a gift from Nephele (Cloud, the queen of Thebes, the house of god) to her two children, Phrixus and Helle, just as their earthly stepmother, Ino, was preparing to sacrifice them to Jupiter. Jumping on its back they made their escape. God appeared as a cloud to protect the Children of Israel during their wilderness wanderings following their exodus or escape from Egypt. Two children, like the two fishes, are under sentence of death. Their only safety is holding on to Aries, the Lamb with the Golden Fleece.

Alas, Helle, lost her grip and fell into the sea at the place immortalized in her honor, the Hellespont (Helle's Pond or Sea). Perhaps this refers to the Antediluvian Church drowned in the Flood of Noah for rebellion against the offers of deliverance in the Ark of safety. Or maybe the Jewish Church in its rejection of Jesus the Christ as their Messiah. Or it might represent "the falling away of apostasy (*2 Thessalonians 2:3*) of the Early Church in their compromise with pagan customs, diluting the pure gospel in a sea of worldly corruption. "The waters which thou sawest are peoples, and nations, and multitudes, and tongues." *Revelation 17:15*.

Phrixus held on and eventually arrived in safety to Colchis, the city of refuge.

> "Here is the patience of the saints, here are they that keep the commandments of God, and the faith of Jesus." *Revelation 14:12*.

In every age, there has always been a faithful remnant remaining loyal to God amid apostasy and rebellion, always clinging to the Lamb of God in their journey to the citadel of salvation.

Aries was ultimately sacrificed to Jupiter in place of Nephele's children. Christ died once for the sins of the world. He was destined to do so "from the foundation of the world." *Hebrews 4:3*. We are purchased, not with silver or gold, or even Golden Fleece, but with the spotless blood of the Lamb of God, who yielded Himself up for us, dying the death that was ours that we might have the life that was His.

Cassiopeia

A woman, strikingly beautiful, seated in queenly dignity on a throne above the Arctic Circle is Cassiopeia—The Beautiful, The Enthroned. She holds a palm branch, symbol of victory, in one hand and with the other arranges her hair in glorious anticipation. On her right hand is the crowned King, holding out his scepter toward (as Albumazer called her) "the daughter of splendor, the glorified woman."

Her throne is formed by four stars of the third magnitude. More impressive are the unusual number of star clusters plus a binary, a triple, a double and quadruple star in this extraordinary constellation. On the evening of November 10, 1572 a star appeared in this constellation surpassing the brilliance of all others. But after dominating the sky for sixteen months, it suddenly faded from view. Star names include:

Shedar	"Freed"
Ruchbah	"Enthroned"
Dat al Cursa	"Seated"

Cassiopeia is regarded as the mother of Andromeda. Thus Paul comments that the heavenly Jerusalem "is the mother of us all." *Galations 4:26*. She was famous for her perfect beauty, fairer than Juno and the envy of all the sea nymphs. "Thy renown went forth among the heathen for thy beauty; for it was perfect through my comeliness." *Ezekiel 16:14*. Jesus presents to himself "a glorious Church, not having spot, or wrinkle, or any such thing; but... holy and without blemish." *Ephesians 5:27*. She is seated on a throne, as the saints will be during the thousand years when John "saw thrones and they sat upon them,... and they reigned with Christ." *Revelation 20:4*

Cetus

Leviathan, a great sea-monster, covers more celestial real estate than any other figure in the sky. This is the beast which the sea-god sent to devour Andromeda. One star in its neck, Mira, is one of the most variable stars known. As bright as the second magnitude, it may fade out of sight once every 300 days and once remained invisible for four years.

Cetus, the Rebel, is held at the neck by the double bands attached to the Fishes. One of its stars, *Menkar,* means "the chained Enemy." It's second brightest star is *Diphda,* "the Overthrown." Job chapter 41 depicts Leviathan as a beast not subdued by man, but here we see it bound. And *Revelation 20* tells of a time when the dragon would be bound by a great chain in a bottomless pit for a thousand years. Isaiah telling of the same event wrote: "The Lord with His sore and great and strong sword shall punish Leviathan the piercing Serpent even Leviathan that crooked Serpent, and He shall slay the Dragon that is in the sea." *Isaiah 27:1.* The same power that upholds the Fishes, binds rebellious Cetus.

Perseus

Perseus, Perses or Perets, the Breaker. *Micah 2:12,13* prophesies that "the Breaker is come up before them." The Lamb, breaks the seals in *Revelation 5*. He who rules with a rod of iron breaks His foes as a potter's vessel and dashes them to pieces. The figure in this Decan stands with one foot on the Milky Way, wearing a helmet and sporting winged feet, he holds a sword in his right hand and the head of the Gorgon in his left. The star by his left foot is *Atik,* "He who breaks." Other stars include: *Al Genib,* "the One who carries away," and *Mirfak,* "Helper."

Perseus was the son of the divine Father and came upon Danae in the form of a shower of gold. As soon as he was born he was thrown along with his mother into a chest and cast adrift on the sea. But Jupiter had fishermen rescue them, transport them to the king where they were entrusted with the care of the temple of the goddess of wisdom.

Soon Perseus became a favorite of the gods for his genius and great courage. Then came the great feast of the king at which everyone was expected to make a presentation. Perseus decided to deliver the head of Medusa, the only Gorgon subject to mortality. The other two, like Medusa, were covered with impenetrable scales and all three had fused their bodies together. They had tusks, yellow wings and heads sprouting serpents instead of hair. They were so horrible, that anyone who chanced to gaze upon them would turn to stone. Pluto, learning of Perseus' ambition, lent him his helmet which would render him invisible. Minerva contributed her polished buckler, and Mercury chipped in wings for his feet and a diamond sword. He flew off to the tangled Gorgons, careful to only look at them through the reflection of his shield. Fortunately both Medusa and all her serpent appendages were dozing. With a single blow, he lopped off the monster's head, grabbed it and flew off with his prize in hand. For such a deed he was granted immortality into the celestial hall of fame, taking his place in this Decan forever holding the grizzly head.

But during his return trip from this escapade, he spotted the beautiful Andromeda chained to the rocks about to be devoured by a sea-monster. Swooping down, he promised to rescue her if she agreed to become his wife. She did so he did. Perseus broke her chains, thrusting his diamond sword into the attacking monster. Phineus tried to prevent their marriage, but Perseus thrust the Medusa in his face and poor Phineus looked and turned to stone.

Revelation 12 tells of a child threatened with destruction from the time of His birth by a great red dragon.

Medusa (trodden underfoot) contains as its principal star *Al Ghoul,* "the Evil spirit," is also a variable star, like *Mira,* changing every three days over a period of only three and a half hours from a second magnitude to fourth magnitude. Other stars are *Rosh Satan* (Satan's Head) and *Al Oneh* (the Subdued).

Perseus, the Breaker, cuts off Medusa's head, puts Leviathan in bonds, and lifts Andromeda to Cassiopeia's heavenly throne.

Taurus,
The Bull

Fierce, terrible, and now extinct, the *Reem* was at one time thought to be an ancient reference to the rhinoceros. It has even been translated unicorn, but was in fact a wild ox or bull. Originally it was much larger, approaching an elephant in size. It was never domesticated, a fact established in *Job 39:9* "Will the reem be willing to serve thee, or abide by thy crib?"

The reem was distinguished for it massive horns, a characteristic applied to Ephraim and Manasseh, the two sons of Joseph, who would wield the inherited power of Egyptian royalty. *Deuteronomy 33:17*. Jesus chose the same symbol when He stands up to defend His people, for whom He appears as the Lamb of God. He is the Red Heifer, the sacrificial Bull. He is Taurus, first of the final four symbols.

Three sets of four divide the celestial circle, the Divine Dozen, the Zodiacal Twelve.

1. The Seed of the Woman
2. The Church
3. The Judgment

Revelation 14:7 speaks of "the hour of God's judgment." More commonly, we find references to the great judgment "day." But the time of judgment is not limited to a mere 24 hour period. Scripture clearly describes the vast extent of God's Judgement. Peter informs us that judgment "begins at the house of God," *I Peter 4:17* that is, consideration is first directed to the church and those who have placed their faith in the Saviour and demonstrated their loyalty before heaven. Daniel speaks of a time when "the judgment was set and the books were opened *Daniel 7:13* and when the Son of Man comes in the clouds of heaven to receive his kingdom and dominion. *Daniel 7:10*.

John describes a similar scene of judgment when the saints shall "reign for a thousand years" *Revelation 20:4* on thrones. Paul asks, "know ye not that we shall judge angels?" *I Corinthians 6:3*

In Hebrew, Arabic, Syriac, Latin, and Greek, Taurus means the Bull. The brightest star found in the Bull's eye is Al Debaran, the Captain. Situated directly opposite Scorpio, Taurus rises as the scorpion retreats.

> "Then the indignation of the Lord is upon all nations,
> and His fury upon all their armies:...
> He hath delivered them to the slaughter.
> Their slain also shall be cast out,...
> and the mountains shall be melted with their blood.
> The **unicorns** shall come down...,
> and the **bullocks** with the **bulls**,
> and their land shall be soaked with blood.
> For it is the day of the Lord's vengeance,...
> and the year of recompenses for the controversy of Zion." *Isaiah 34:2,3,7,8.*

This is when the Lord "comes out of His place" to punish the wicked for their iniquity, *Isaiah 26:21* when He shall "no longer keep silence," *Psalm 50:3* when He will "perform His strange act." *Isaiah 28:21*. The Lord is "long suffering, not willing that any should perish." *II Peter 3:9* But the time will come when the proclamation is made: "He that is holy let him be holy still, he that is filthy let him be filthy still." *Revelation 22:11*. Then His forbearance ceases. Then "the Lord Jesus shall be revealed from heaven with His mighty angels, in flaming fire taking vengeance on them that know not God, and that obey not the Gospel." *2 Thessalonians 1:7, 8*. Then "the kings of the earth, and the great men, and the rich men, and the chief captains, and the mighty men...hide themselves in the dens and in the rocks of the mountains" and call "to the mountains and the rocks 'Fall on us, and hide us from the face of Him that sitteth upon the throne, and from the wrath of the Lamb:

for the great day of His wrath is come; and who shall be able to stand?" *Revelation 6:15–17*

Orion, First Decan

The mighty hunter raises a great club high above his head and clutches the skin of a slain lion. With one foot raised to crush the head of his enemies, he wears a valiant sword from his belt. "I will send for many hunters, and they shall hunt them from every mountain, and from every hill, and out of the holes of the rocks; for mine eyes are upon all their ways: they are not hid from my face, neither is their iniquity hid from mine eyes." *Jeremiah 16:16–18*

Here is *Orion,* the Brilliant, Swift. God says to Job that Orion is invincibly girded: no one can loose his bands. *Betelgeuse* burns brightly on His right shoulder. It means The Coming Branch. *Rigel,* first magnitude star, shines from His lifted foot. It means "The Crushing Foot." Three stars form the glittering belt, called by various names: The Three Kings, Jacob's Rod, the Ell and Yard. "Righteousness shall be the girdle of His loins, and faithfulness the girdle of His reins." *Isaiah 11:5. Bellatrix* (Suddenly Destroying) is located in Orion's right chest, another consistent appellation of the invincible Avenger.

Mythology tells an account of Orion as the greatest hunter in the world, who could walk the sea without wetting his feet, surpassing in strength and stature all other men. He claimed to have conquered every beast on earth. But a scorpion, hearing of the claim, inflicted a mortal wound on his foot. Diana invoked the gods to grant him immortality and place him in the heavens opposite Scorpio.

Jesus was indeed the greatest of all men. He came into this world to "destroy him that hath power over death, that is, the devil." *Hebrews 2:14*

Eridanus, Second Decan

From under the foot of Orion, flows a long and tortuous river named *Eridanus*, "River of the Judge." Myth records a tale when the chariot of the Sun lost control and threatened to destroy earth in a fiery conflagration. During the crisis, Phaeton was struck by a thunderbolt, and thrown into this river where he perished, burned and consumed by the heat that rendered much of earth inhabitable.

Revelation and Daniel describe a river flowing from the throne of God Who is the Judge of heaven and earth. "His throne was like the fiery flame, and His wheels as burning fire. A fiery stream issued and came forth from before him...The judgment was set, and the books were opened." And Daniel "beheld even till the beast was slain, and his body destroyed, and given to the burning flame." *Daniel 7:9–11* "Our God shall come, and shall not keep silence: a fire shall devour before Him, and it shall be very tempestuous round about Him." *Psalm 50:3* "A fire goeth before Him, and burneth up His enemies round about Him." *Psalm 97:3–5* "His lips are full of indignation, and His tongue as a devouring fire: and His breath as an overflowing stream...the breath of the Lord, like a stream of brimstone, doth kindle it." *Isaiah 30:27–33* "His fury is poured out like fire." *Nahum 1:6*

Though Revelation speaks of a "lake of fire" and a "river of life," Eridanus is the fate of the presumptuous Phaeton, that bears him away to "the lake which burneth with fire and brimstone, which is the second death." *Revelation 20:14*

Auriga, Decan Three

A mighty man seated on the Milky Way, holds a cord in one hand, and cradles a mother goat in his other arm above two little kids resting on his lap and sheltered by his massive hand. This enigmatic figure was a puzzle to the Greeks who apparently ignored its inclusion in their mythological structures. They called him *Haeniochos*, the Chariot Driver.

Modern atlases designate him as the Wagoneer. Yet both terms oddly fit this picture of a man preoccupied with tending goats.

The absurdity is resolved by considering the Latin version of his name, *Auriga,* Shepherd.

Here is the Good Shepherd who laid down his life for the sheep. *John 10:11.* The Zodiac of Dendera illustrates Auriga holding a scepter forming the head of a lamb on one end and the figure of a cross on the other. The she goat clings to his neck. The cords are the same we saw in the hand of the Lamb and Cepheus, the dual bands that guide and protect his children while restraining and binding their enemies. It is the amalgamation of justice and mercy. *Habbakuk 3:2*

"Trust in the Lord, and do good; so shalt thou dwell in the land, and verily shalt thou be fed. For evildoers shall be cut off; but those that wait upon the Lord, they shall inherit the earth. For yet a little while, and the wicked shall not be: yea, you shall diligently consider his place, and it shall not be. For the Lord loveth judgment, and forsaketh not His saints; they are preserved for ever." *Psalm 37:3, 9, 10, 28*

The dominant star, *Capella,* marks the heart of the mother goat who looks back upon the Bull, "the terrible."

> "Behold, the Lord will come with strong hand, and His arm shall rule for Him…He shall gather the lambs with His arm, and carry them in His bosom, and shall gently lead those that are with young." *Isaiah 40:10,11*

This agrees with the Chaldaic name for the star in his right arm: *Menkalinon,* "the Band of the Ewes."

The day of judgment is coming which "shall burn as an oven" when the "proud and all that do wickedly shall be stubble and the day that cometh shall burn them up," and "leave them neither root nor branch." *Malachi 4:1* But the Good Shepherd extends His open arms with the invitation to all, "Come unto me all ye that labor and are heavy laden and I will give you rest." *Matthew 11:28*

> "Unto you that fear my name shall the Sun of Righteousness arise with healing in His wings: and you shall go forth and grow up as calves of the stall; and you shall tread down the wicked; for they shall be ashes under the soles of your feet in the day that I do this, saith the Lord." *Malachai 4:2,3*

The United Gemini

Here are two young companions embraced in congratulatory celebration of a battle won. One holds up a great club, the other a bow and arrow, both emblems of war brandished in the aftermath of victory. Images of returning troops riding atop tanks and jeeps, waving their arms in the air with shouts and cries of triumph are today's version of The Twins.

Mythology placed these two as sons of Jupiter among the Argonaut crew in pursuit of the Golden Fleece. During their endeavor, both warriors demonstrated exemplary heroism. One with impressive prowess and artful exercise of spear and bow. The other for unparalleled equestrian expertise. On return from their successful mission, they rid the Hellespont area of all pirates and other maritime predators. Paul, on his voyage to Rome, sailed from Melita following the shipwreck aboard a vessel named in honor of these two inseparable heroes. "We departed in a ship of Alexandria, which had wintered in the isle, whose *sign* was *Castor* and *Pollux* [the Twin Brothers]" *Acts 28:11*

Held in the highest esteem, Greeks and Romans alike would swear by their names in indication of the most profound integrity and truth. The custom survives today in the phrase, "by Gemini."

During the Calydonian Hunt the pair fought and slew Amycus, the giant son of the sea god, when he threatened them and the other Argonauts. During this conflict they were aided by lightning bolts from Jupiter who also granted them power over the winds and the waves of the sea.

The Egyptian zodiac of Dendera shows this sign as a man and woman walking hand in hand. Some have identified this as Adam and Eve. But the Old Coptic name for this sign, *Pi Mahi*, means "the final union" or the "completed consummation" indicating the Lamb and His bride, Christ and His Church, chosen before the foundation of the world, betrothed from the beginning, are now ready for their marriage supper.

In the left foot of the southern figure is *Al Henah*, a conspicuous star whose name means "The Wounded." It was the seed of the woman whose heel would be bruised. In his head resides a star named *Pollux*, meaning "Ruler," "Judge," "the Toiling Deliverer." In the center of his body shines *Wasat*, "Seated" or "Put in Place."

The southern figure is also the one who holds the club to bruise the head of the serpent. Egyptian astronomers referred to him as *Horus*, "the Coming One," "the son of light," "the serpent slayer," "the son of the sun," "the mighty avenger." These names correspond to the Babylonian god *Murdoch* or *Merodach*, "the great Restorer." These parallel the *Redeemer*, the *Saviour*, the *Messiah* who is promised to restore justice, to set at liberty those that are bound.

But these two figures are really one. As a man and wife become one flesh, and as the Father and Son are one, so is the union of Christ with His church. We are the branch, He is the vine. But He is also called the Branch. They are two and yet they are one, He is in us and we are in Him. Throughout scripture, the children of God experience the same events, receive the same assurances, speak the same words, rejoice in the same promises. Christ is called the Son of God. He promises that we, too, who believe in Him shall be given "power to become the sons of God." "Behold, what manner of love the Father has given unto us that we should be called the sons of God." *I John 3:1*

The northern twin is called *Castor* or Apollo, "The Coming Ruler" or "Judge" who punishes and destroys the wicked, who has the spirit of prophecy, who sings the song of Moses and the Lamb, who protects and keeps the flock.

Lepus the Hare

A giant rabbit depicts the first decan, positioned under Orion. *Arnebeth* in its Arabic form, implies the meaning of an enemy. Orion was said to be especially fond of hunting hares. The Egyptian zodiac displays a serpent for this decan, trodden under the foot of Orion or caught in the claws of a hawk. Another name is *Bashti-Beki,* "the Confounded Offender." Its stars have interesting names: *Nibal,* "the Mad;" *Rakis,* "the Caught;" *Sugia,* "the Deceiver."

Lepus indicates the impending doom of Evil's reign. As the Church is lifted on high to its destined union with Christ, the empire of darkness receives a stunning blow, harbinger of its soon demise. As the royal announcement is made, "The marriage of the Lamb is come!" He who is called Faithful and True rides from heaven on His white horse, leading the armies of heaven to make war with the Beast and the kings of the earth. *Revelation 19:7, 11, 14.*

Sirius, Canis Major, the Dog

The Hound of Heaven, a wolf, stands ready to pounce on Lepus, his prey. The Denderic Zodiac shows an Eagle or hawk attacking a serpent. The name is the origin of titles, *Sir* and *Sire,* meaning "Guardian," "Victorious Prince." The Egyptian form included *Naz-Sir* which is preserved in the popular name, *Nazir,* meaning "The Sent Prince." The Rod which Isaiah promised would come from the stem of Jesse is called *Netzer,* translated "Branch." Jesus grew up in an obscure village by the name of Nazareth. "He came and dwelt in a city called Nazareth, that it might be fulfilled which was spoken by the prophets, He shall be called a Nazarene." *Matthew 2:23.*

The stars of this decan are:

Mirzam	"Ruler"
Muliphen	"Leader, the Chief"

Wesen	"Shining, Illustrious, Scarlet"
Adhara	"Glorious"
Al Habor	"The Mighty"

Curious names for any ordinary dog, but fitting epitaphs to the Saviour who champions in defense of His bride.

Canis Minor, the Second Dog

Following at a distance, smaller, the third Decan befits the saints, who follow the lamb withersoever He goes. *Rev. 14:4* The Egyptian Zodiac shows a man with an Eagle's head, a mirror of the great Eagle in the first Decan, *Sirius*. The name they apply is *Sebak*, "Conquering."

At the center of the constellation is the principal star, *Procyon*, "Redeemed." The second star, *Al Gomeiza*, "Redemption."

The betrothed of Christ live by faith in experiencing the sweet communion with the True Vine, *I Corinthians 13:12* looking through a glass darkly, *Hebrews 10:20* reaching by hope through the veil into the inner Sanctuary. But soon we will meet our Lord face to face, we will see the King in all His glory, joined at last in complete union, joint heirs with Christ, *Romans 8:17* caught up to meet the Lord in the air, *I Thessalonians 4:17* as a Bride prepared for her Husband. *Revelation 21:2.*

Cancer, The Crab

"I will multiply thy seed as the stars of the heaven, and as the sand which is upon the sea shore;" *Genesis 22:17*

A giant crab is shown in nearly all Zodiacs for this sign including the Parsi, Hindu and Chinese versions. The exception is the Egyptian star map where the picture of *Scarabaeus*, the sacred beetle, is represented.

But considering the crab, notable parallels are found between this gangly crustacean and the redeemed heirs of Abraham's Seed "according to the promise." Both are born of water. The crab sports numerous legs as does the church of Spiritual Israel in its multitudinous members. As the crab undergoes repeated moltings so the church develops in putting off the old man while putting on the new man, not to be conformed to this world but transformed by the renewing of our Spirit, a prelude to putting off the corruptible in order to put on immortality at the last trump when death is swallowed up in victory. *Colossians 3:9, 10; Romans 12:2; 1 Corinthians 15:54*

While the crab has powerful pincer claws that are capable of grasping firmly with amazing force, so God's chosen have "lain hold of the hope set before" *Hebrews 6:18* them and have "chosen the good part that shall not be taken away." *Luke 10:42*

Some have questioned whether the Egyptian beetle could possibly have been the original sign for this constellation. If this were the case, the application is just as poignant. The beetle begins life as a grub that spends its existence beneath the ground, limited in mobility, deprived from the bright world above to simply grow and wait on Nature's schedule. So we bide our time in this life, in a world of darkness, obliged to toil and certain to suffer, arraigned with fear and assailed by doubt.

But the day finally comes when change is eminent. The larva is encased in a chrysalis, enshrouded in a state of suspended animation. Movement, feeding, and all apparent activity ceases. It is intermission time, a death to the old life, a bridging transformation to a new life to come. So it is with death, the sleep of which Jesus spoke. "Lazarus is asleep but I must go to awake him from sleep." *John 11:11*. "Weep not, for the damsel is but asleep." *Luke 8:52*. Those who sleep in the safe arms of Jesus are freed at last from the cares and wants of this life; free to wait on Him Who will call them by name, "Awake, awake, ye that dwell in dust... and the earth shall cast out the dead" *Isaiah 26:19* "And many of them that sleep in the dust of the earth shall awake." *Daniel 12:2* "Marvel not at this: for the hour is coming, in the which all that are in the graves shall hear his voice, and shall come forth; they that have done good unto the resurrection of life." *John 5:28,29*

The beetle was the all-time national favorite motif in ancient Egypt. Its form was stamped on ornaments and official seals, fashioned into jewelry, and engraved on tombs. Many have wondered why such attraction was given to a bug. But few have considered the important role this figure played in the Egyptian Zodiac as the star-sign of the celestial perfection, transformation from things earthly to things divine.

Praesepe

An unusually brilliant nebulous cluster occupies the center of this constellation. Named for both Hebrew and Arabic meanings that include the concepts of "a Multitude of Young Offspring," or "the Innumerable Seed." Moses referred to this in his comments on the tribe of Issachar as possessing "the abundance of the sea and of treasures hid in the sand." *Deuteronomy 33:18,19*. Jacob prophesied of Shiloh who was to come, who would "bind His foal to the vine, and His ass's colt to the choice vine." *Genesis 49:10–15*. Some ancient star maps indeed show two asses in the location of Cancer that have been perpetuated by the Greek myth that these two animals assisted Jupiter in his victory over the giants.

Egyptian astrologers called this sign *Klaria*, meaning "the Fold." *Khan* is Hebrew for "a traveler's resting place." *Ker* has the meaning of "embraced" or "held within encircling arms." Thus Cancer means "rest secured." The principal star is *Acubens*, "the shelter;" other stars are *Ma'alaph* (assembled thousands) and *Al Himarein* (kids or lambs). This, then, is the place of eternal rest for the flock of God.

Ursa Minor

The first decan is the Lesser Bear, a sad misnomer for a figure that is depicted as a long tailed animal which is very unbearlike. The original name for the dominant star in this decan is *Dubah* (*Dober* in Hebrew) which means a sheepfold or corral for domestic animals. But this word was apparently confused with Dob, the word for bear.

The Danes and Icelanders called this decan, Thor's Chariot. The Britons called it Arthur, after their great hero. It contains seven stars called the *Septentriones*. The Arab astronomers dubbed these *Ogilah*, "wheels." They have also been called "Charles's Wain" or "Wagon." These seven have also been connected with the seven stars or churches in Christ's right hand as shown in the book of Revelation. The entire number of stars in the constellation is 24, a reference to the 24 elders, the Church of the Firstborn.

Star names include:

Kochab	"Waiting the Coming"
Al Pherkadain	"The Calves, the Young, the Redeemed"
Al Gedi	"The Kid, the Chosen of the Flock"
Al Kaid	"The Assembled"

But the principal star is the Pole Star or *Al Ruccaba*. The Greeks called it *Arktos*, meaning "an Ark, a haven for the saved."

Ursa Major

Originally called the Great Sheepfold, *Al Naish*, by the Arabs.

The chief star is *Dubah*, "herd or fold."

Next in brightness is *Merach*, "the flock."

Others include:

- *Cab'd al Asad*, "multitude of the assembled"
- *El Acola*, "the sheepfold"
- *Al Kaiad*, "the assembled"
- *Alioth*, "the ewe mother"
- *El Kaphrah*, "the protected redeemed"
- *Dubheh Lachar*, "the latter herd"

Job spoke of "Arcturus and his sons," as the seven stars of the Great Bear.

The Dendera Zodiac shows this decan as a swine, the enemy of the Serpent, holding a plowshare, that tears up the ground, destroying serpent domiciles.

Argo, Decan Three

Argo was the mysterious vessel that bore the argonauts on their expedition to recover the Golden Fleece. The Fleece was once the property of our original human parents, a mythical symbol of their holy innocence in Eden. But through deceit, the Serpent stole the Golden Fleece from Adam's hand, who forfeited his dominion over Earth to the prince of this world. According to the tales of Homer, the Fleece was guarded in the grove of Mars, fierce god of justice at Colchis, the citadel of atonement. No human could ever retrieve it. But finally Jason, the Atoner, the Healer, organized an expedition under His leadership to brave fierce trials and sufferings to take the precious prize and return home victorious. The Argo is the old ship of Zion shown in the stars as it lands safely home in its heavenly port.

Chief star in this decan is *Canopus*, the helmsman who died from the serpent's bite.

Others include: *Sephina,* "multitude or abundance of good" (Moses of Issachar *Deuteronomy 33:19*).

Tureis, "the treasure secured"

Asmidiska, "the travellers released"

Soheil, "what was desired"

The Dendera Zodiac features a mighty ox with a cross hanging about his neck. Even in ancient times, the cross was a symbol of immortality and eternal life. The figure's name is *Shes-en-Fent* which means "Rejoicing over the Serpent."

> "There does remain a rest for the people of God."
>
> *Hebrews 4:9*

> "Let not your heart be troubled…In my Father's house are many mansions. I go to prepare a place for you…I will come again, and receive you unto myself, that where I am there ye may be also."
>
> *John 14:1–3*

> "The ransomed of the Lord shall return, and come to Zion with songs and everlasting joy upon their heads; they shall obtain joy and gladness, and sorrow and sighing shall flee away."
>
> *Isaiah 25:10*

> "And there shall be no more death, neither sorrow, nor crying, neither shall there be any more pain: for the former things are passed away."
>
> *Revelation 21:4*

On the imperishable stars these truths have hung and pictured their confident faith across the many millennia. Even today they speak to us of comfort and courage upon whom the ends of the world have come.

Leo,
The Lion of the
Tribe of Judah

The Mother of all documents lay seemingly unreachable within the hand of Almighty God. The scroll was sealed completely and perfectly with seven royal seals. Its contents would remain forever closed to probate; inheritance would be eternally denied to the helpless heirs if a qualified administrator of the debt-burdened estate could not be found. The fate of an entire race rested on the chance that somewhere in the vast universe a legal council would step forward with the necessary credentials to access the impounded title-deed. Prospects looked bleak, indeed, hopeless. John, overwhelmed with the immense odds, broke down in shameless sobs.

Then he heard that voice easing his anxious cries: "Weep not. Behold, the Lion of the tribe of Judah, the Root of David, hath prevailed to open the book and to loose the seven seals." *Revelation 5:5*

Here is the last of the celestial signs—a Lion, the king of beasts, majestic and noble, strong and powerful, fearing nothing. Stealthy yet nimble, this mighty cat strikes terror in the hearts of men and beast alike with the thunder of its roar.

Jacob, on his death bed, pronounced a blessing on his son Judah as the leader of his brethren, out of whom the kings of Israel would be born. David, the second king of Israel, well demonstrated the lion qualities of a mighty man of war. Yet the prophecies spoke of One Who would be the son of David, Who would rule all nations with a rod of iron. But when Jesus came, and all eyes turned to Him as the long-awaited Messiah, He acted as "the Lamb of God slain from the foundation of the world." *Revelation 13:8*. To many this was an intolerable disappointment.

Even when John heard the voice inviting him to look at the Lion, his first glance revealed "a Lamb as it had been slain with, seven eyes and seven horns." *Revelation 5:6.* In His avenging role against the enemies of His people, Jesus appears as the mighty Lion; to those He has redeemed, He is the sacrificial Lamb.

> "I will be unto them as a lion. I will rend the caul of their heart. I will devour them like a lion."
>
> *Hosea 13:7,8*
>
> "Wait upon me, says the Lord, until the day that I rise up to the prey (when) I assemble the kingdoms, to pour upon them my indignation."
>
> *Zephaniah 3:8*
>
> "The Lord will roar from Zion, and utter His voice from Jerusalem; and the habitations of the shepherds shall mourn, and the top of Carmel shall wither. Will a lion roar in the forest when he has no prey?" *Amos 1:2; 3:4,8*

All celestial globes, all star maps, all known Zodiacs present the image of a lion in the sign of Leo.

Thoroughly aroused, the Lion-Lamb approaches the Majesty of His Father *Revelation 5:7–10* and takes the sealed document amid shouts of glory and exultant praise that shakes the universe to its core. As He breaks each seal, planet Earth shudders in violent convulsions. War and revolution, bloodshed, famine and death strike terror in the hearts of even the bravest Hollywood superhero. Mountains are wrenched from their foundations. Islands shift and sink out of sight. A final desperate attack is mounted by the forces of Evil against the sole remaining children of God who wait in loyal trust for their Redeemer. One moment they huddle as prey before the slaughter; the next their assailants become the prey of Leo as He fiercely pounces on the hosts of Armegeddon.

The star names in Leo's constellation are deeply significant:

Aryeh	"He who rends"
Al Sad	"The One who tears and lays waste"
Pimentekeon	"One who pours out rage and tears asunder"
Leon	"He who leaps with consuming fire"
Regel	"Crushing feet" (The brightest star located in Leo's chest)

Psalm 91:13 Describes this crushing defeat of God's enemies, the serpent, the asp and the dragon trampled under the feet of the Lion.

Denebola	"The Judge who comes with haste"
AlGiebha	"The exalted"
Zosma	"The shining epiphany"
Minchir al Asad	"Tearing the Destroyer"
Deneb al Eced	"The coming Judge who violently shakes"
Al Defera	"The Defeat of the enemy"

The wrath of the Lamb, the "Stone cut out without hand," the Lion of the tribe of Judah is the story told in the sign of Leo. *Revelation 6:16; Daniel 2:24; Revelation 5:5*

Hydra

Stretching a full third across the sky's sphere, Hydra, the great Serpent flees before the Avenging Lion. But Leo, with His great claws extended, leaps upon the snake's neck and certain to crush its head. The final blow, long before promised in Eden at the hand of the Woman's Seed, is now to strike with deadly power.

Hydra's mythical fame originated in the Lernaean lake, home to the world's first sea monster with one hundred heads. A unique feature of this beast was its amazing ability to not only regenerate a severed head, but duplicate it as well. Unless a would-be vanquisher was careful to not only whack off a head, but sear the writhing stump with fire, two new heads would immediately sprout.

> "Raising a hundred hissing heads in air;
> When one was lopped, up sprang a dreadful pair."

This is exactly what happened when Hercules made his initial attempts at ridding the world of this horrible super snake. He finally discovered that a simple cauterization of the amputated neck would prevent cephalic regeneration. Though Hercules, according to Greek legend, employed a red-hot iron, Revelation indicates that it is clearly impossible to destroy this evil creature except it be transported from the lake it had infested to a lake of fire.

"Hydra," which means "Abhorred," contains a number of named stars:

Al Phard "The Separated, Excluded, Removed"

Minchir al Sugia "Tearing to pieces the Deceiver"

Crater, the Cup of Wrath

The cup is Scripture's symbol for the receptacle of both blessing and suffering. Sitting at the table prepared for God's flock, David saw his cup running over with goodness and mercy. *Psalm 23:5*. This blessed experience is made possible only because the Good Shepherd *John 10:11 gave* up His life for the sheep and drank the cup of suffering. After "he took the cup and gave thanks" in a toast at the Last Supper, Jesus said "This fruit of the vine...is my blood of the new testament." Moments later He was praying, "O my Father, if it be possible, let this cup pass from me." But the Father's will would prevail. When Peter drew his sword and de-eared Malchus, the high priest's servant, Jesus said: "Put up your sword: the cup which my Father has given me, shall I not drink it?" *Matthew 26:27,28,39. John 18:11.*

Jesus drank the cup, all of it, to the dregs so we don't have to. He experienced the agony of eternal separation so we can experience the joy of eternal life in His presence. But it's our choice to accept the Gift. We may choose to let Him fill our cup to overflowing, to drink our fill of the water of life, to come to the waters and buy wine and milk without money and without price. *Isaiah 55:1*. Or we may reject the offer of divine substitution and drink the cup of indignation ourselves. *Revelation 14:10*

> "In the hand of the Lord there is a cup, and the wine is red; it is full of mixture; and He pours out of the same: but the dregs shall all the wicked of the earth wring out and drink." *Psalm 75:8*

> "Upon the wicked He shall rain burning coals, fire and brimstone, and a fiery tempest: this shall be the portion of their cup." *Revelation 11:6*

> "The same shall drink of the wine of the wrath of God, which is poured out without mixture into the cup of His indignation; and he shall be tormented with fire and brimstone in the presence of the holy angels, and in the presence of the Lamb." *Revelation 14:10*

The cup in Leo's second Decan lies directly on the Serpent's writhing body. In fact, the same stars share both the form of Hydra's body and the cup's bottom rim. Undiluted, unmixed with water, liquid wrath will pour from God's cup upon the Evil Hydra in the final lake of fire.

Corvus, the Raven

Solomon, though not known particularly as a prophet, did prophesy in *Proverbs 30:17* that "the eye that mocks his father, and despises his mother, the ravens of the valley shall pick it out, and the young eagles shall eat it." Solomon's father, David, was a preliminary symbol of Judah's Lion. When confronted with Goliath, the giant from Gath, David prophesied too. "I will smite you, and take your head away from you; and I will give the carcasses of the Philistine host this day to the fowls of the air and to the wild beasts of the earth." *1 Samuel 17:46*. And he did. When the final Lion comes pouncing down from heaven, riding His white horse, leading the hosts of heaven to deliver the wrath of God, an angel stands in the sun and calls out to all the fowls and birds of prey to come and feast themselves on the slain bodies of God's enemies. *Revelation 19:17,18*.

Corvus sinks its talons into Hydra's body, and tears at *his* flesh with its beak. The eye of the raven is a star named *Al Chiba*, "the Inflicted Curse." Another star is *Minchir al Gorab*, "the Tearing Raven."

The subtle Snake, the cunning Deceiver, the wily Serpent has coiled himself around this world, injecting all with his deadly poison. But his doom is certain. The Lion will crush his head, the Raven will tear *his* flesh, and the Cup of fiery wrath will cremate his lifeless carcass. Reduced to ashes, "trodden under foot" by the redeemed of all ages, Hydra will never again raise his ugly head. *Malachi 4:3*

> "There shall be no more death, neither sorrow, nor crying, neither shall there be any more pain: for the former things are passed away." *Revelation 21:4.*

The Twelve Celestial Signs and Their Decans

Virgo To Leo Summary

Virgo—A virgin conceives and bears a son, Immanuel, the Branch of the stem of Jesse, the Desire of all Nations.

Virgo

Coma, the Infant, the Branch, the Desired One

Centaurus, a centaur with arrow piercing its victim

Arcturus, the great Shepherd, Harvester, holding rod and sickle

Libra—Who is destined to pay the final price, measuring out the Redeemer's life for that of his chosen...

Southern Cross, under Centaur

Centaur's Victim, slain, pierced to death

Northern Crown, prized by the Serpent

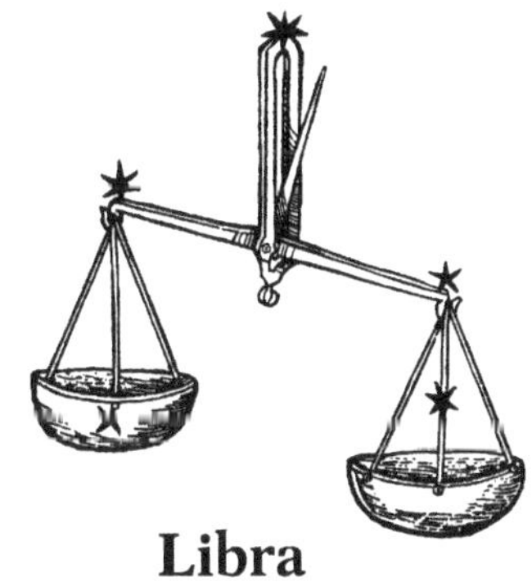

Libra

Scorpio—By a poisonous wound in the heel of the Redeemer, as the Scorpion is crushed underfoot.

Scorpio

Serpent, struggling with Ophiuchus

Ophiuchus, stung in one heel by the Scorpion, crushing it with the other

Hercules, wounded heel, but foot over the Dragon's head

Sagittarius—Rising as a conqueror, terrible as an army with banners, he shoots his arrows into His enemies.

Lyra, a Lyre held by an eagle in triumph

Ara, the burning Altar spilling its coals toward earth

Draco, the Dragon coiled about the Pole

Sagittarius

Capricorn—As the Sacrificial Goat takes the sins of His people, dying to give life to a multitude of fish...

Capricorn

Sagitta, the Arrow on its mission of death

Aquila, the Eagle, pierced and falling

Delphinus, the Dolphin leaping from the sea

Aquarius—Swimming in a river of life as Christ pours water, His Spirit, upon the thirsty ground.

Southern Fish, drinking in the stream poured by Aquarius

Pegasus, white winged horse, swiftly galloping with good tidings

Cygnus, the Swan, bearing the sign of the cross

Aquarius

Pisces—Two fish, churches with a common legacy, held and controlled with cords of love, held by the...

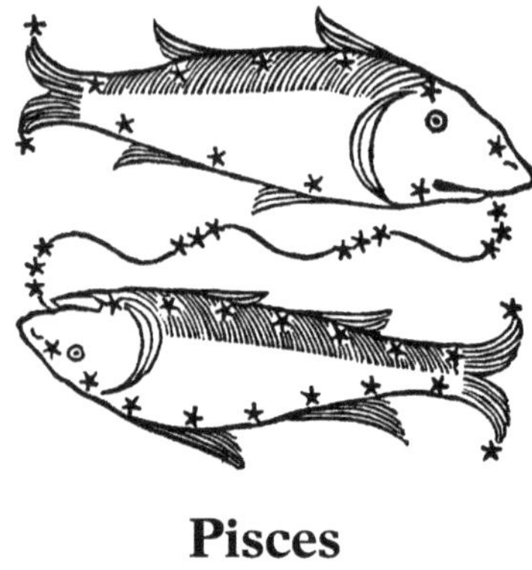

Pisces

Rod, held by the Lamb, holding up the Fishes and holding down Cetus

Cepheus, the great Victorious crowned King, standing on the polestar

Andromeda, woman in chains, threatened by Medusa's cranial serpents

Aries—The Lamb of God Who takes away the sins of the world and returns again as the Shepherd-King and

Cassiopeia, the enthroned woman

Cetus, the Sea-Monster, bound by the Lamb's rod

Perseus, mighty warrior with winged feet, sword in hand, carrying the monster's head

Aries

Taurus—The Sacrificial Bull, the Red heifer, coming to save His people and Judge their enemies.

Taurus

Orion, the glorious Prince, sword on belt, his foot upon the Serpent's head

Eridanus, Orion's tortuous River

Auriga, the Shepherd carrying goats on his left arm, holding cords in his right hand

Gemini—The Lamb is at last joined with His Bride, Christ with His Church, two and yet one.

Lepus, the angry Serpent under Orion's feet

Sirius (Canis Major), the Great Dog, the coming Prince

Procyon (Canis Minor), the Second Dog following Sirius

Gemini

Crab—The Church, like a molting crab is transformed while slinging fast to the Hope set before it while...

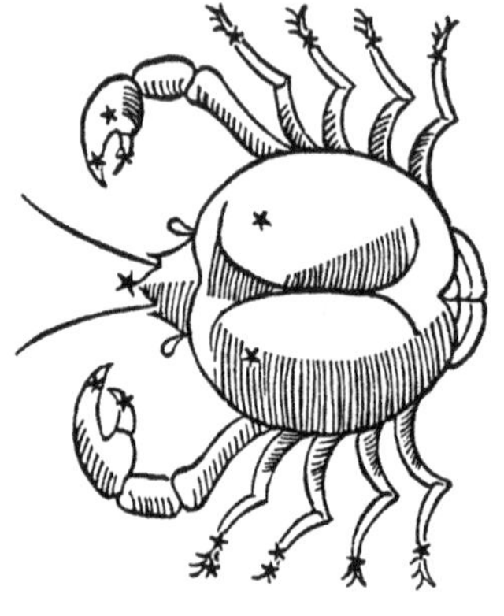

Cancer

Ursa Minor, the Lesser Sheepfold, enclosing the Pole

Ursa Major, the Greater Sheepfold, near Arcturus, keeper of the flock

Argo, the Ship, bearing the traveling Argonauts returning with the Golden Fleece

Leo—The Lion-King majestic and avenging, tramples the fleeing serpent under His feet.

Hydra, the fleeing Serpent, trodden underfoot by the Lion

Crater, the Cup of Wrath upon the Serpent

Corvus, the Raven, bird of doom, tearing the Serpent

Leo

"Thy faithfulness shalt thou establish in the very heavens." Psalm 89:2

TEACH Services, Inc.
PUBLISHING

www.ingramcontent.com/pod-product-compliance
Lightning Source LLC
Chambersburg PA
CBHW060543100426
42742CB00013B/2426

* 9 7 8 1 5 7 2 5 8 1 3 9 5 *